MW00643381

ALABAMA

THE PROGRAM

A Curated History of the Crimson Tide

AARON SUTTLES

TRIUMPH
BOOKS

Library of Congress Cataloging-in-Publication Data is available upon request.

This book is available in quantity at special discounts for your group or organization. For further information, contact:
   Triumph Books LLC
   814 North Franklin Street
   Chicago, Illinois 60610
   (312) 337-0747
   www.triumphbooks.com

Printed in U.S.A.
ISBN: 978-1-63727-103-2
Design by Preston Pisellini
Page production by Patricia Frey

To Stephanie and Grayson, who showed me what a home is.

CONTENTS

PART 3 Building the Teams

PART 4 Traditions

PART 5 Player Profiles

Foreword

GREAT IS SO OVERUSED A WORD THAT IT HAS LARGELY LOST meaning. When excellence is as relentless and methodical as a metronome, it numbs us, or at the very least lulls us into expecting it as normal. But there is nothing routine or normal about the history of Alabama football. Greatness is never routine, no matter how customary such a display seems. *Greatest?* Now you stir the blood, you invite subjectivity, and arguments ensue.

The debate should be over, for there is no rational opposition to calling the Nick Saban era not only the greatest in the storied history of the Crimson Tide but also the greatest in college football history. Under Saban's guidance, Alabama has won games and claimed championships at an unprecedented level over an unparalleled length of time. Alabama is the standard by which others are measured—a machine that insists its parts fit in order to crush the souls and spirits of all who dare to stand in the path. That is a school of thought with which I differ. The Process isn't fitting the next widget into the juggernaut; it's enlightening players about the mutually beneficial relationship of creating value for themselves (to repeat Saban's oft-used phrase) while being part of something bigger than themselves.

That is the secret: the people. The stories. The relationships. The decisions. I suspect Nick Saban would've won big no matter what. But take, for instance, Julio Jones's decision to come to Tuscaloosa as part of Saban's first full recruiting class. It kicked the Process into overdrive. There is no one player, in my judgment, who has embodied excellence and passed it down to future Alabama players more than Julio.

But this dynasty was built on a host of personalities. There is Mark Ingram, a native of Flint, Michigan, whose fandom in his post-Heisman days make him revered among the so-called Gumps. AJ McCarron brought swagger. Rolando McClain and Reuben Foster delivered an edge. Jonathan Allen and Dont'a Hightower imposed their will and demanded teammates come along. No player was ever more a reflection of his coach than Minkah Fitzpatrick. Derrick Henry and DeVonta Smith brought transcendent brilliance. Tua Tagovailoa and Bryce Young revolutionized the perception of Alabama quarterbacks. Mac Jones's fearlessness even extended to tweaking Saban in practice as the scout team quarterback before leading perhaps Alabama's greatest team.

There's that word: *greatest*. How is it truly measured? From my perspective, it might be measured by wins. But it is built on the power of personalities and the stories surrounding them. That is the foundation of college football's greatest dynasty and one of the great dynasties in all of sports. Few have greater insight into this than Aaron Suttles. In his own inimitable way, Aaron will deliver never-before-heard stories that will give you insight into the rich history of Alabama football. Soak this up. Never get bored with excellence.

—Rece Davis
ESPN *College GameDay*

Introduction

I REMEMBER THE EXACT MOMENT I FELL IN LOVE WITH college football. For most things, my memory is not so good, especially for a journalist and writer. I forget names at a historic level; truly, my capacity to remember a stranger's name after first meeting them is impressively bad. However, there are certain things that have imprinted themselves in my mind that I'll always remember. Such as the time I stumbled across my dad's box full of VHS tapes containing old college football games. As a young boy, this was heaven to me.

I bet I watched those games 100 times apiece. These were older games—before my time, really—that only had one thing in common: at least one team featured in each was from the SEC. The 1982 Sugar Bowl particularly held my interest. I guess it was watching Herschel Walker and Dan Marino slug it out that captured my young imagination. I rewound that Marino touchdown pass for the win over and over again.

Another tape held the 1982 Cotton Bowl, a 14–12 Texas win over Alabama. Texas scored all their points in the fourth quarter, and with time running out and pinned deep in their own territory, they had the punter run out of the back of the end zone for a safety. My young mind always thought it dumb to take a safety to decrease your lead to 2 points with 48 seconds remaining. Didn't Texas head coach Fred Akers realize that a field goal would beat him? "What was he thinking?" I've asked myself more times than I care to count.

I kept myself entertained for hours in my dad's basement with that treasure trove of college football history. I can close my eyes and still see my dad's VCR remote control. It was a Mitsubishi and had a round knob on it. Instead of hitting a rewind button, I could just turn the knob to the left to rewind or to the right to fast-forward.

College football was always how my dad and I bonded. It was how we understood each other. It was the only thing either of us ever felt comfortable talking about with the other. The truth is, we never really knew each other.

My mom and dad divorced when I was a child. He moved to Chattanooga, Tennessee, and I stayed with Mom in Fort Payne and then in Leighton, where my mother's side of the family lived. I didn't see my dad much, but I knew he loved college football, and I felt like if I liked it enough too, then we could share something that could cross the divide. I'd go stay with him on occasion, and I could talk to him about what those games were like to watch in the moment. Why did Texas take that safety? How good were Marino and Walker back then?

My dad was a huge Alabama fan. He didn't go to school there; instead a career in the air force awaited him. There, as a sergeant, he became an engineer, a career he thoroughly loved. This was a man who loved to tinker, loved to build computers—he loved his gadgets. But he loved Alabama football the most, and that's what started my love affair with college football.

I was accepted into the University of Alabama out of high school, but my dad lived in Chattanooga, working for the local

CBS affiliate there, and he asked me if I would come there and enroll at the University of Tennessee at Chattanooga. That meant casting aside my plans for the opportunity to really get to know my father. I jumped at the chance.

One of the first weeks I was there, he asked me if I wanted to go the Alabama-Vanderbilt game. Going to my first college football game with my dad? This was too good to be true. But that Saturday morning he got called into work, and we had to postpone. He knew I was disappointed, and I'll never forget what he said to cheer me up: "Don't worry, we've got plenty of opportunities to go see a game." Two weeks later he died. I withdrew from UT-Chattanooga and eventually made my way to the University of Alabama. Not the most conventional route, but it was mine.

I've thought about that month I spent with my dad before he died a lot over the years. We never really knew each other, not really. We never really knew how to communicate other than through college football. Maybe that's why the game is such a part of my life now. Maybe that's why I devoted my professional life to documenting the game. I never set out to cover Alabama football for a living. I wanted to report on Major League Baseball. God had other plans, though.

I've reported on Alabama football since 2007. I don't know if it's fate or pure coincidence that my journey has paralleled Nick Saban's tenure at Alabama. Covering the greatest college football coach of all time during the greatest dynasty in college football history at the program my dad loved—well, it doesn't seem like a coincidence to me. At least that's not what I let myself believe.

I wonder what my dad would think of my career. I think he would have been happy about how hard I worked to get to this point in my career. I think he would pepper me with questions every day about what's going on with his favorite college football team. I like to think he'd be proud.

Covering Saban's Alabama teams has taken me places a boy from Leighton, Alabama, doesn't dare dream of. I've covered nine national championship games. I've covered multiple Heisman Trophy winners. I've covered multiple games that the president of the United States attended.

And that's how I've arrived at this book. The opportunities I've been provided over the years have given me access to some incredible moments in college football history. I wanted to share some of the coaches, teams, players, and stuff I've learned about this program in my 15 years covering it. I hope you enjoy it.

PART 1

THE COACHES

1

Nick Saban

WHAT CAN YOU SAY ABOUT NICK SABAN THAT HASN'T already been said? Probably not much, but his excellence— which has been the subject of several books and multiple documentaries—requires intense study. He developed the renowned "Process" that is the definition of everything in his program; his way of speaking inspires catchphrases.

For a man who eats the same Little Debbie Oatmeal Creme Pies for breakfast and the same turkey salad every day for lunch, Saban is anything but boring. He's a man of routine, but that doesn't mean he gets stuck in his ways. Anything but. Imagine a man in his 60s—and in Saban's case now, in his 70s—who got to the top of his industry and is unafraid to alter what got him there.

Usually when someone reaches the top of their profession, they never veer from the formula that got them there. That was Saban for the first half of his tenure at Alabama. He was a coach who built his teams on defense and power running. That's not to say he didn't value the passing game, but there was a certain physicality to Saban's early Alabama teams that had his signature on them. In the middle of that run, in the midst of that dominance, college football shifted its rules to favor the offense.

Way back in 2012, Hugh Freeze was the first-year Ole Miss head coach who implemented a style of offense that wasn't frequently seen at the time. His teams ran a play, got to the line as quickly as possible, and ran another play, oftentimes before the defense could adjust or make substitutions. The week following Alabama's 33–14 win over the Rebels—a game in which Ole Miss held the ball for only 25:01 but ran more plays than the Crimson Tide (68–64)—saw more than a few raised eyebrows from the way Freeze had called the game, and afterward Saban was left wondering where college football was headed.

Saban's response to these new hurry-up, no-huddle offenses came in a now-famous statement during a press conferences about this new direction in college football. He uttered a combination of words that has become his catchphrase, used time and time again in college football when change is happening. It's come to signify that while Saban is questioning whether a change is the best thing for the game, he'll make the change and dominate within that new reality.

"I think that the way people are going no-huddle right now, that at some point in time, we should look at how fast we allow the game to go in terms of player safety," Saban said. "The team gets in the same formation group; you can't substitute defensive players; you go on a 14-, 16-, 18-play drive; and they're snapping the ball as fast as you can go, and you look out there and all your players are walking around and can't even get lined up. That's when guys have a much greater chance of getting hurt—when they're not ready to play. I think that's something that can be looked at. It's obviously created a tremendous advantage for the offense when teams are scoring 70 points and we're averaging 49.5 points a game.... More and more people are going to do it. I just think there's got to be some sense of fairness in terms of asking, 'Is this what we want football to be?'"

"Is this what we want football to be?" It's become a running joke among Alabama fans whenever a change occurs. Because Saban seemingly issues a warning, then he makes whatever change is occurring, bringing it into his program, and begins to dominate with the new rule.

The rise of the hurry-up, no-huddle offense was the impetus that completely changed the way Alabama played offense. Saban knew his way of playing—big, thudding defense with a power running game—was on its way out. He had to adapt. He did so with a new offensive philosophy outside his comfort zone. He brought in Lane Kiffin. Kiffin gets his own section in this book, but his hiring is just one example of how Saban adapted.

Kiffin was hired to install a new offense, and he did. It wasn't a change that happened overnight. Because although Saban got with the times and installed a new offense, it would take some time to recruit the players to run it. In Kiffin's first season, he started a converted running back at quarterback. Then he had a pro-style passer in Jake Coker the next. In his third and final season as the Crimson Tide's offensive coordinator, Kiffin started Jalen Hurts. You can see the evolution in three years' time, from the body styles the program recruited to the level of quarterback it could now attract to the abundance of wide receivers. Give Saban the credit for recognizing it was time to make a change and for hiring Kiffin, which was always viewed as an odd marriage.

"Well, Lane did a fantastic job for us when he was the offensive coordinator, and I don't think that he probably gets— we made a tremendous change when Lane came in, and Lane had always been the same...philosophy-wise as we were in terms of pro-style football," Saban said. "And because of what Ole Miss—and it's ironic that [Kiffin is] at Ole Miss now—had done and beaten us several times running the spreads, running the RPOs, running the screens and things that are difficult to defend because of the rule of blocking downfield when the ball is thrown behind the line of scrimmage—and we weren't utilizing some of those things, which I thought put us at a disadvantage, and Lane really hadn't done much of that stuff either.

"So when he came in, I said, 'Look, we want to change this. You need to research this. You're smart. We can do this.' He actually did implement that and was the first one to sort of change how we did things on offense. It enhanced our opportunity to score more points.... Because we're a little different, a lot of people have sort of wondered what the relationship was, but we never really had a bad relationship, because [there] was always a lot of mutual respect for the kind of play caller he was, the kind of coach that he was, and the job that he did. I actually said...when he went to Florida Atlantic that Lane will be a better head coach than even he is an assistant because he has those kinds of qualities. Obviously, he hasn't disappointed in the job that he did there or the job he's done at Ole Miss. So none of this is a surprise to me. And I...can only say from my perspective how much respect I have for him as a coach."

The upgrade helped the offense become one of the most explosive in college football. The offensive coordinators have come and gone, but the results remain largely the same. After Kiffin, it was Brian Daboll. Alabama won a national championship with him. Then it was Mike Locksley, who got Alabama to the national championship game in 2018. Then it was Steve Sarkisian, who helped Alabama win a national championship in 2020. This past year it was Bill O'Brien, who got Alabama to the national championship game.

The style of offense attracted better skill position players too. Jalen Hurts, Tua Tagovailoa, and Mac Jones were all NFL starters during the 2020 season. Before them, Alabama didn't have a full-time starter at quarterback for an NFL team, although John Parker Wilson, Greg McElroy, and AJ McCarron had made NFL rosters. The wide receivers have followed suit with elite talents such as Calvin Ridley, Jerry Jeudy, Henry Ruggs III, DeVonta Smith, and Jaylen Waddle all taken in the first round of the NFL Drafts. (Amari Cooper was too, but he was recruited before the change in offensive identity.)

Elite running backs have been part of the formula since Saban's arrival in 2007, and they weren't forgotten about as the offense shifted focus to the passing game. Kenyan Drake, Josh Jacobs, Damien Harris, and Najee Harris are all on NFL rosters. (Mark Ingram and Derrick Henry are too, but they were recruited before the change in offensive identity.)

Not only is Saban a master at assembling talent, but he also seems to thrive when making difficult personnel decisions. For instance, when his team was floundering in the 2018 national championship game against Georgia, Saban made the difficult decision to bench starter Jalen Hurts and insert Tua Tagovailoa. The decision paid off, as Tagovailoa led a legendary comeback for the national title in overtime. Saban's decision, though, led to an off-season quarterback controversy for the 2018 season. Tagovailoa won the job, and Saban was able to keep Hurts in the fold until the following season, when he transferred to Oklahoma. It was a balancing act of a season for Saban, and when the roles were reversed in the SEC Championship Game and Tagovailoa was injured and Hurts was inserted into the game, Saban had instilled confidence in Hurts for just that moment. It worked, and Hurts led a comeback win over Georgia. In an emotional postgame interview, Saban proclaimed how proud he was of Hurts for what he'd endured during the regular season going from a starter to a backup.

The Hurts-Tagovailoa relationship was widely speculated about and awkward, but both were mature in how they handled it.

"I'd say our relationship has grown," Tagovailoa said. "Our communication with how we see things now, I think, has grown a lot. When I go in on 7-on-7, he's kind of watching in the back. When he goes in, I watch in the back. Sometimes we question each other, like, 'Why did you do this, why did you do that?' The communication with us has been really good. I think we've been improving a lot as an offense, within not only our running game but also our passing game while we're communicating to each other as well. It benefits both of us. And Mac Jones as well. I'm happy that Mac Jones got his first touchdown this season. It's exciting."

Who would have thought that Alabama—who before Saban's arrival last had a quarterback start and win an NFL game in 1987, when Jeff Rutledge did it—would have three future NFL QB starters on the sideline at the same time? All three of those guys were Heisman Trophy finalists, although Hurts did it after he transferred to Oklahoma.

That's part of the Saban legacy now. Alabama quarterbacks are viewed completely differently now than before his arrival. Before Tagovailoa was drafted fifth in the 2020 NFL Draft, the last Crimson Tide quarterback to get drafted in the first round was Richard Todd, who was selected sixth overall in 1976.

It's not lost on anyone that Tagovailoa and Jones were Heisman Trophy finalists and then Bryce Young became the first Alabama quarterback to win college football's top individual award in his first year as a starter. Much like with wide receivers and running backs, Alabama has become a program that attracts top-flight quarterbacks.

McCarron was a highly regarded recruit, but he was from the state of Alabama. Saban went to Texas to get Hurts, to Hawaii to get Tagovailoa, to Florida to get Jones, and to California to get Young. He also just signed another highly regarded quarterback in the recruiting class of 2022 in Ty Simpson from Tennessee.

There's no guarantee that Simpson will be the next guy, but Saban was high on him during the recruiting process. "Ty Simpson is certainly someone that we recruited a long time, know a lot about, is made of the right stuff, and certainly has a lot of talent and ability," Saban said.

If you're looking for other metrics to help put into context what Saban has done at Alabama, think of his ever-growing coaching tree. Two of his former assistants who are now head coaches—Jimbo Fisher and Kirby Smart—have national championships. It's probably no coincidence that those are the only two former assistants to actually beat Saban.

After defeating Saban and Alabama for the 2021 national title in January 2022, Smart was effusive in his praise for his longtime boss and mentor. "I mean, he doesn't lose many national championship games when he has that time to prepare. And he does a really good job," Smart said. "So to do it and beat them, that's special. But also I have a tremendous amount of respect for him, the way he runs his program. And [this is] really probably one of the best jobs he's ever done with his team, because they were really young at some positions. And I think they've got the best player in college football in Bryce Young, and I saw it firsthand on the field in the SEC championship. But to do what he did this year, with that team—I told him after the game, I said, 'I really believe that this was probably the best job you've ever done.' And people don't understand that. Media don't respect that because they didn't win the national championship. But the job he did with that team? Incredible. Incredible."

Other former Saban assistants who are Power 5 head coaches include Billy Napier (Florida), Mario Cristobal (Miami), Kiffin (Ole Miss), Geoff Collins (Georgia Tech), and Sarkisian (Texas).

Cristobal is one of the bright up-and-coming coaches in the country. He said being on the Alabama staff felt like getting an advanced degree. "The knowledge I gained by sitting in that think tank of a coaching room with all those other assistant coaches—how do you say thank you for that type of experience?" Cristobal said. "I've said it so many times. It's like getting a PhD in coaching. I'm so thankful. Coach Saban has been tremendous as a mentor. He's done this for well over 40 years now, and he kind of knows that the industry moves fast and that livelihoods and families and futures are at stake. At the end of the day, he is very supportive anytime a staff member has an opportunity to improve anything for their family and their careers. He really is. [I'm] indebted forever for the most incredible coaching experience anyone can ever imagine. I mean, the Crimson Tide family took me in, and never did a day go by when I didn't pour my entire heart and soul into it."

That's one of the more remarkable untold facets of Saban's approach: He's been able to attract top assistants into his program, some of them former head coaches, and then they leave and erode Alabama's foundation little by little.

The team's success and Saban's structure helped Kiffin and Sarkisian get their careers back on track after bumpy exits at Southern California and formed them into viable head coaching candidates again. Others, such as Smart and Jeremy Pruitt, went from being career assistants to head coaches after Saban's tutelage. When those coaches left, they cherry-picked personnel within the Crimson Tide program. After a few years, that erosion eats away at a program; some who might have been candidates at Alabama become assistants at other programs. Saban doesn't mind that because he wants his employees to get career opportunities, but it does make it more and more difficult to build a coaching staff when positions become available. He doesn't begrudge those getting opportunities because for him it's an opportunity to bring something new to his program.

Saban addressed this idea when he talked about his new coaching staff in the off-season following the 2020 season, including a pair of former NFL coaches in Bill O'Brien and Doug Marrone. "First of all, the staff that we had last year did a phenomenal job, and we're happy for those that got better opportunities. Several guys got head coaching jobs, and one guy got a coordinator job. So we're excited about the opportunities that they got for themselves," Saban said. "I'm also excited about the people that we're able to hire. So a lot of questions have been asked about these NFL guys [O'Brien and Marrone]. [Sarkisian] and Kyle Flood were NFL guys when we hired them too.... And I think when it comes to offensive coordinator, quarterback development, you need knowledge and experience, and I think I think offensive line is the same kind of deal. The other coaches that we were able to hire are great position coaches that are good recruiters, so we're excited about the staff that we have right now. But we also have a tremendous amount of appreciation for the job that last year's staff did as well.

"There'll be new energy, new enthusiasm, new ideas in terms of how we can improve what we are doing, but we've never reinvented the wheel here when we hired new people. We've just tweaked what we do to feature the players we have, and that's what we'll try to do with this group."

When you think about the 15 years Saban's been coach at Alabama and all that's transpired, it requires a long view. Sometimes when you're too close to something, you lose perspective of what you're seeing. Saban took over a rebuilding job of a once-proud football powerhouse program. It took him until just his second season to have the team ranked No. 1 in the country. In every season that's followed, his teams have been ranked No. 1 at some point in every season. It's truly mind-blowing.

But as tough a job as it is to rebuild a program, those who've done it say that maintaining is the far more difficult job. As Saban publicly remarked to New England Patriots coach Bill Belichick, "When you get to the top of the mountain, you become the mountain." Meaning you become the target for another program to climb and overtake.

Saban has mastered both the rebuild and the maintaining. Every member of each Alabama recruiting class who stayed in the program has won a national championship. Saban's list of accomplishments is so deep and varied that you become somewhat numb to them when you read them one after another. Such is his greatness.

He's done this during a time when there have been rules enacted specifically to limit a program's longevity at the top. There was the rule the NCAA came up with that prohibited head coaches from going on the road for spring visits, which was dubbed the Nick Saban Rule for Saban's ability to outwork other coaches on the recruiting trail. The tilt of the sport to be more offensive was certainly not a direct shot at Saban and his program's success, but it inarguably affected it. He adapted to make the rules favor him.

When the SEC went against its own rule not to allow players to be immediately eligible for in-conference transfers, Saban eventually relented but warned that the potential for NFL-style free agency was right around the corner. "I think the spirit of the transfer portal in and of itself is a positive thing for players," Saban said. "I think when we started with the transfer portal, it was a mechanism for players to be able to say 'I'm transferring,' so everybody knows that I'm transferring, so if that creates opportunities for me to go different places, then that's a good thing for the player. The issue with the transfer portal is we've gotten very liberal in giving people waivers, so when we do that, it becomes free agency, which I don't think is good for college football. I don't think it's good for fans."

Saban looked clairvoyant when he accepted Tennessee transfer Henry To'o To'o at linebacker and Ohio State transfer Jameson Williams at wide receiver; they were two of the Crimson Tide's better players in 2021.

That wasn't the first time he predicted what would happen. When college football moved away from the BCS model and toward the College Football Playoff to determine a national champion, he knew what was coming in regards to a lack of interest overall in bowl games. "I have mixed emotions about expansion," Saban said. "I always said way back when, when we started this whole playoff thing, even when we started just having a two-team national championship game, that this would reflect poorly on players' interest in playing in bowl games. I think that's come to fruition with the number of guys that opt out and don't play. One of the great things about college football is that a lot of players got rewarded, got a lot of positive self-gratification for having a good season by being able to go to a bowl game. There was a lot of interest in all those games; there were some great matchups. We have some great bowl partners in college football. Now that we have a playoff, even though it's four teams, all the attention goes to the playoff, and the importance of bowl games has been minimized with fans [and] players. I don't know if that's good or bad. If we expand, that's going to further diminish the importance of bowl games. Maybe those two things can't coexist. If they can't coexist, then having a bigger playoff would probably be a good thing."

It seems only a matter of time before the leadership in college football expands the playoff and the SEC is determined to protect its own interest with regards to automatic qualifiers and how that could affect the number of SEC teams who could get into a playoff. What Saban is saying and has always been saying when it comes to dramatic changes to the sport is that there are always unintended consequences.

Because of his foresight and his leadership abilities, many have opined that Saban is the exact kind of mind that should be tending to the health and future of college football as its commissioner. There is no college football commissioner, only conference commissioners and university presidents, and they shape the sport's future through varied biased perspectives. There isn't one voice looking out for the sport, just a bunch of voices looking out for their own interests.

But Saban has no interest in being a commissioner of college football. He's too much of a competitor, and being a part of a team is in his DNA. And although he would be perfect for the job, he seems quite content with the job he has. The 70-year-old coach seems to genuinely enjoy doing what he's doing. Even in one of his most trying seasons, the 2021 team reached the national championship game despite myriad shortcomings. It was a young and immature team in many ways, and it was an undisciplined team too. Yet it had a lead in the fourth quarter of the national championship game despite all that. That's largely due to Saban's coaching. He seemed to enjoy watching the team grow. It wasn't easy. At some points that team must've driven him crazy. But it was a championship team, claiming the program's 29th SEC title even when not many thought it was possible.

But they lost the College Football Playoff National Championship 33–18 to Kirby Smart–coached Georgia 33–18 on January 10, 2022. The loss only gave Saban an opportunity to reveal the depth of his humanity; he seemed authentically happy for his former assistant for winning a national championship.

And in the postgame press conference, Saban stopped it momentarily so he could brag on Alabama's two best players and its two best leaders in the worst moment of their amateur careers to date. As quarterback Bryce Young and outside linebacker Will Anderson stood to make their way off the stage, Saban stopped them. "I'd like to say something. Can I say something?" Saban began. "These two guys sitting up here— they're not defined by one game. They played great for us all year. They were great competitors, great leaders on this team, and they contributed tremendously to the success of this team. And we would not be here without them. And both of them take responsibility for the loss, but both of them contributed in a lot of ways, in a positive way, to giving us a chance to win and a chance to be here to have an opportunity to win. So I just want to thank them for that and let everybody know how proud I am of these two guys."

Saban showed a side of himself that season that even endeared him to people who were not Alabama fans, even people who quite frankly didn't like him before. I've heard more from fans who used to hate Saban about how much they like him now. A great deal of the reason for that is that Saban showed a softer side of himself. When he couldn't get the team to perform like he wanted because it was younger and inexperienced, he made the decision to publicly be more positive with them. He knew that constantly jumping down their throats wasn't going to get the desired effect. So he went the other way.

He also showed a softer side of himself when I got caught holding my infant son during a midweek press conference via Zoom. My son was about a year old, and I didn't feel confident enough to put him in his playpen so I could conduct an interview, so I held him and prayed that my wife would show up before it was my turn to ask a question. My prayers went unanswered, and I tried to ignore the fact that I had an infant on my left shoulder as I asked a question about linebacker Henry To'o To'o.

Saban responded by having a good sense of humor about the situation and asking if he "finally got to meet the boss." That video has been viewed more than a million times and was on ESPN and went across the sporting landscape. People instantly connected with how he handled the situation of a poor sportswriter caught in an uncontrollable situation. Saban was gracious and funny. He converted a lot of people that day.

That's where Saban sits at the moment. That doesn't mean that this new soft side is here to stay. I suspect with a pretty veteran team coming back for 2022, we'll see a louder Saban, especially if press conferences go back to in-person. It's hard to yell at a reporter over Zoom but not hard at all in person.

It just goes to show how adaptable Saban is in every aspect of his job. Some still carry the incorrect opinion that Saban is too rigid and set in his ways. In some ways, perhaps—the mantra "Do your job" is never going to change. But in the important ways, the ways that predict success and the continuation of that success, Saban has been, is, and will always be evolving.

2

Lane Kiffin

When all is said and done in the Nick Saban era of Alabama football, there will be much to celebrate and much to examine. One thing is for certain: from an entertainment perspective, there was no better period than the stretch from 2014 to 2016, when Lane Kiffin served as offensive coordinator. Not coincidentally, it was also a stretch of three straight SEC titles for the Crimson Tide program. The team won a national championship in 2015 and came excruciatingly close to another in 2016.

There were bumps along the way too—Kiffin's sideline ass-chewing from Saban, the firing before the national championship game against Clemson at the end of the 2016 season, and more.

The highs and the lows—that's what makes Kiffin's three-year stint the most all-around entertaining period of the Saban era. Kiffin had been suddenly discarded on the trash heap after being fired and left on a tarmac by Southern California in 2013, and he just as suddenly hooked up with the greatest coach in college football, probably the one coach who was the diametric opposite of him in terms of personality and perception. Those things have never mattered much to Saban. He's given many a coach another chance, leading to lots of jokes about Saban and Alabama being a sort of rehabilitation clinic for wayward coaches. But it worked until—again, suddenly—it didn't at the very end.

Saban is able to compartmentalize better than most. He accepted Kiffin for what he was, a great offensive mind and an elite play caller. For my money, he's the best play caller of the Saban era, although Steve Sarkisian was elite with all that talent in 2020 as well. On second thought, let's call it a tie. Still, Kiffin turned a converted running back in Blake Sims into one of the most efficient quarterbacks in the country in 2014. He did so by being able to communicate with Sims from the sideline. Before Kiffin, every UA offensive coordinator under Saban operated from the coaching booth upstairs in stadiums. Realizing that one of Kiffin's gifts was being able to dissect a defense in real time and counter it, the decision was made that Kiffin would call plays from the sideline. He was a savant at doing so. There's no better example of that than during the LSU game in Baton Rouge in 2014.

After somehow getting the game into overtime with a last-minute drive down the field for a game-tying field goal, Kiffin made the ultimate adjustment when he saw how LSU lined up defensively. With wide receiver DeAndrew White lined up inside to the right and wide receiver Christion Jones on the outside to the right, Kiffin called for a rub play to create room for White. Jones ran a slant inside and White ran a fade to the outside. The route created enough space for Sims to loft a fade to White for the eventual game-winner. It was a moment that proved how good Kiffin was at adjusting on the fly in real time and being able to clearly communicate that to a one-year starter at quarterback in Sims.

Kiffin was many things: He was talented. He was good. And he knew it. Which led him to being cocky and arrogant. It was all part of the Kiffin experience at Alabama, and what a ride it was.

It wasn't all smooth sailing on the field for Kiffin, for example. It was rumored that he was butting heads with offensive line coach Mario Cristobal. It's safe to say that the two weren't the best of friends. There was also a near mutiny at halftime of the College Football Playoff game against Ohio State in the Sugar Bowl when the offensive line felt they weren't running the ball enough with Derrick Henry and T. J. Yeldon. They'd rushed only 12 times in the first half, and the guys up front wanted to run the damn ball and weren't shy in expressing that in the locker room.

And sometimes things were bumpy for Kiffin off the field. He twice got left by team busses after games—once after the national championship win over Clemson to end the 2015 season and another time after media day for the 2016 Peach Bowl in Atlanta. There was also the time he missed the bus for a scrimmage and was spotted running down Bryant Drive and attempting to get inside Bryant-Denny Stadium. Saban keeps a tight schedule, and not even the offensive coordinator is able to delay it.

There's also no denying that part of Kiffin's appeal is his personality. He likes attention. He welcomes it. Sometimes it's unwanted attention, but most of the time it's carefully crafted to attract the most attention possible. While at Tennessee and Southern California when he was the head coach, he sort of became the first TMZ college football coach. He was a good-looking guy who was easily recognizable. He was also good for a spicy quote to jab other programs, and sometimes coaches and players.

While the coach at Tennessee, Kiffin was said to have told Alshon Jeffery during his recruitment that if he chose to sign with his home-state South Carolina Gamecocks, he would end up pumping gas for the rest of his life like all the other players from his state who had gone to South Carolina.

He was brash early in his career, and that created an atmosphere in which people, even casual sports fans, took notice of him. That's continued throughout his career. There's an interest in Kiffin that is difficult to explain to the unanointed. Seemingly everything he does creates headlines. And that attention sometimes spills over into his personal life. For instance, he had an alias in Tuscaloosa that he was alleged to have given out to women: Joey Freshwater. Seriously. Look it up. He had a special section behind the bar at the popular Tuscaloosa college bar Innisfree.

But no one would care about his off-the-field exploits if he couldn't coach. Without that, he'd be just a sideshow, a traveling circus freak. But he *can* coach, and that's what makes his time in Tuscaloosa all the more interesting. Under Kiffin's direction, Alabama produced three consecutive SEC Offensive Player of the Year winners—Amari Cooper (2014), Derrick Henry (2015), and Jalen Hurts (2016)—and three straight SEC titles.

And now that he's back in the SEC—especially in the SEC West, at Ole Miss—it's made his and Saban's relationship the subject of much attention. If you listen to Saban and Kiffin speak about each other, it sounds like a well-rehearsed mutual-admiration society. In many ways, it really is: Saban has described on multiple occasions how Kiffin took Alabama's offense and built it into the Death Star it is today, and Kiffin has often spoken about how Saban saved his career and gave him a new platform after his tarmac firing from USC.

That's about the extent of their relationship outside of football. They're not going to swap Christmas cards or be dinner companions outside of SEC obligations, and they won't be vacationing together. One compliments the other's football acumen and vice versa, and that's where it stops.

And there's nothing wrong with that. By and large, reporters are complicit in creating storylines in which we overvalue former coworkers being real-life friends off the field. It's cliché and overdone. There's a certain happiness fans find in coaches of their favorite teams chumming it up after hours. Remember when Jimbo Fisher and Will Muschamp and their families shared a vacation home? We couldn't get enough of it. It seemed like someone brought it up every time one of their names was mentioned.

Saban and Kiffin are two coaches who used to share meeting rooms and sidelines who are inextricably tied to each other but will never share a relationship beyond that. Now they're coaches on opposing sidelines, and both would like nothing more than to put an *L* on the other every time they meet.

There's also the fact that their personalities seem to be the polar opposite; they are night and day. While Saban will sometimes unleash a joke or comedic story that seems out of left field, you almost expect those things from Kiffin. Saban, the stalwart veteran coach unwilling to utter anything but positive remarks about the upcoming opponent, versus Kiffin, who seemingly takes any opportunity to needle Saban on social media. Kiffin often uses emojis to symbolize rat poison, a tip of the hat to a famous Saban rant after a win at Texas A&M in 2017 when he compared media hype to rat poison.

And the week of the Alabama–Ole Miss game in 2021, Kiffin held his Monday news conference with a Coca-Cola bottle and a Dasani water bottle on the podium, something that Saban does each week because he's contractually obligated to because of an arrangement between Coca-Cola and the University of Alabama's athletic department. Some around Alabama football felt it was a deliberate troll move because Kiffin hadn't had a Coke bottle at the podium at any point before that season.

And if there's a head coach who uses Twitter to his benefit more than Kiffin, I'd like to meet him. Kiffin does it better than anyone else in the sport. Part of the beauty of that is that he controls his message. Some coaches do press conferences and then let the masses take from it what they will. Kiffin has his press conferences and supplements them with social media. Often funny, sometimes a bit irreverent, and oftentimes trolling. He tweets articles and adds a comment or emoji. Last season, ESPN's Mike Wilbon called Kiffin a "clown" and an "embarrassment." Kiffin responded to it on Twitter twice in two days. During the week of his biggest game to date as head coach at Ole Miss, Kiffin was responding to criticism from a media member via social media. Can you envision Saban even acknowledging such a thing without a question prompting him to do so? Night and day.

That's not to suggest one is a better tactic than the other. Everyone is entitled to protect their reputation and character as he or she sees fit. It just highlights the differences between the two coaches.

While Saban and Lane Kiffin's relationship dates back to 2009, it actually goes back much further between Saban and Monte Kiffin, Lane's football-famous father. Saban, a football junkie, met with the elder Kiffin when Saban was a staff member at West Virginia. "I think Lane's dad was really instrumental in a lot of things," Saban said. "I remember, I think he was at Nebraska way back when I first started coaching...and we went and visited him, and Pete Carroll was actually with him at the time. He was really the first coach, that I remember, that actually coordinated the front-end coverage—where you overshift the front one way and balance the coverage back the other way and tie it together in a way that is very, very effective. Then he gets a lot of credit when he was in Tampa for 'Tampa 2,' and I think he was the first person to do that, and it caused people a lot of issues for a long time. I always had a ton of respect for Lane's dad, Monte. He visited here a few times when Lane was here. I just think he's a wonderful man, and his legacy as a coach is not necessarily because he won a lot of games or was a great head coach, but what he did to impact the game was probably as significant as anybody I know."

The first on-field meeting between Saban and the younger Kiffin came in the fall of 2009 when Kiffin brought his Tennessee team, with Monte as his defensive coordinator, into Tuscaloosa to play Saban and No. 1 Alabama. UA scored only 12 points that day and only secured a victory when nose guard Terrence Cody blocked a field goal as time expired. Sources have said over the years that Saban felt Tennessee was one of the most prepared teams Alabama faced all season on the way to a national championship.

There was also the issue of the headsets that afternoon. During the first half, the Tennessee coaching staff notified officials that the staff's headsets weren't working properly, so the officials, by rule, required that the Alabama staff stop using their headsets too. It made for some comical conspiracy theories after the game. Did those headsets really stop working? Maybe we'll never know.

Kiffin seemed on the verge of building something significant at Tennessee in year one, when Southern California came calling. He accepted and left Knoxville after one of the most bizarre press conferences of all time. But he was fired as the Trojans head coach in the middle of the season, setting up one of the strongest unions between a head coach and an offensive coordinator that we've ever seen. Saban has remained gracious through it all, even after having to fire Kiffin the week before the national championship game in 2017. He's more than happy to acknowledge what Kiffin did to reinvent the Crimson Tide offense. He did so at SEC Media Days in July 2020 before Kiffin's first season at Ole Miss, and he did it again before they faced each other in 2021.

"We made a tremendous change when Lane came in, and Lane had always been the same...philosophy-wise as we were in terms of pro-style football," Saban said. "And because of what Ole Miss—and it's ironic that he's at Ole Miss now—had done [by beating] us several times running the spread, running the RPOs, running the screens, and things that are difficult to defend because of the rule of blocking downfield when the ball is thrown behind the line of scrimmage...I thought put us at a disadvantage, and Lane really hadn't done much of that stuff either.

"So when he came in, I said, 'Look, we want to change this. You need to research this. You're smart. We can do this.' He actually did implement that and was the first one to sort of change how we did things on offense. It enhanced our opportunity to score more points. So he did a really good job, and I think...a lot of people have sort of wondered what the relationship was, but we never really had a bad relationship because this was always a lot of mutual respect for the kind of play caller he was, the kind of coach that he was, and the job that he did. I actually said and told the people when he went to Florida Atlantic that Lane [would] be a better head coach than... an assistant because he has those kinds of qualities. Obviously, he hasn't disappointed in the job that he did there or the job he's done at Ole Miss. So none of this is a surprise to me."

And Kiffin has never shied away from his appreciation of Saban for taking him at his lowest professional point. But because he is who he is, Kiffin always likes to troll just a bit. "[Saban is] certainly not on Twitter, we know that. Now, Linda [Leoni], his assistant, is—probably prints them out, especially the ones that he may not like," Kiffin said. "So he probably does see those. But I think it's all in fun. I think you guys know...how much respect I have for him, how grateful I am for him hiring me and the three years together with him and what that did for my career. But the respect—like I said, nobody's done it like he's doing it, ever."

As much as the two pay lip service to each other, there will also be the famous ending in Tuscaloosa. No. 1 Alabama had just beaten Washington in the Peach Bowl semifinal and was set to rematch with Clemson in the national championship game. But not everyone was pleased with the level of preparation Kiffin had given in the lead-up to the Peach Bowl. Kiffin, like other Alabama assistants before him who were going off to be head coaches, had been given the space to start building his staff for his new job at Florida Atlantic. But the two job responsibilities proved too much for Kiffin, and Saban had to let him go. Saban felt he had no choice and that he owed it to his team, and that doing so allowed Kiffin to get on with the business of being Florida Atlantic's head coach. It was a little more involved than that, but at the end of the day, Alabama parted ways with Kiffin so he could do the myriad things that a head coach must do when taking over a program.

Alabama, with Steve Sarkisian calling the plays, lost that national championship game to Clemson on a last-second touchdown throw from Deshaun Watson. There are many who still feel that if Kiffin had been able to handle both jobs, Alabama would've won its second consecutive national championship with him as the offensive coordinator. Unfortunately, that's something we'll never know.

3

Kirby Smart

THERE'S BEEN AN INORDINATE AMOUNT WRITTEN AND spoken about Nick Saban and Kirby Smart's relationship. That's understandable given the history of the two. Smart was the longtime defensive coordinator Tuscaloosa under Saban, arguably the game's best coach of all time. Anytime two people spend that amount of time together and then split and are still forced to compete with each other, there are always going to be people wondering about the relationship.

The two have both won national championships—Saban seven and Smart one. Smart was the defensive coordinator for four of Saban's titles, and they've both beaten each other for a national championship. Smart stayed at Alabama a long time, waiting for the right time to make the leap to become a head coach. He's been gone a while now, and early on rumors said that Saban and Smart's relationship was bumpy. Let's get one thing straight: It'll never be how it was before, when Smart was on Saban's staff.

And then there are the accusations regarding Smart's behavior on his way out. In the winter of 2015, as he was transitioning away from Alabama, Smart simultaneously served as Alabama's defensive coordinator and Georgia's head coach. Things got weird and feelings got hurt between Smart and the Crimson Tide program he had served for nine years. Time has healed wounds from some of those slights—perceived or otherwise—but history remembers, as does the Alabama fan base no longer enamored with their onetime defensive coordinator.

On his way out the door back then, Smart took a picture of Alabama's recruiting board, which hangs in the inner sanctum of the Alabama football building, and showed it to recruits who weren't necessarily at the top of that board. His message was simple: "Alabama doesn't want you as much as it says it does." The recruiting business is notoriously cutthroat, and coaches do what they have to do to be successful in getting players to their respective campuses, but this instance of negative recruiting felt wrong to those at Alabama, and it left a bad taste in their mouths at the time.

Each of the four times Alabama and Georgia have met since Smart took over the latter's program (2017, 2018, 2020, and 2021—twice), the questions have come. And Saban has answered them the same way every time: He has insisted that just because you compete against someone doesn't mean you can't be friends with him. But the relationship between the two SEC coaches competing for national championships isn't actually as rosy as some would paint it. That doesn't mean the two are hostile to one another, but it does mean they aren't particularly close. Perhaps that has eased over the years, but their relationship isn't as close as you'd think for two men who spent a significant portion of their professional lives together.

Smart has installed the Process 2.0 at Georgia, taking the blueprint from Tuscaloosa and mirroring it in Athens with successful results. Smart just won the Bulldogs their first national championship since 1980, and he did so while becoming the first Alabama assistant to beat Saban. In Smart's six years at Georgia, he's lost and won a national championship to Saban.

Yet for all the successes he's achieved since striking out on his own, it's not unusual for Smart to still call and seek advice from different UA athletic department administrators. Not as frequently as he did in his first couple years in Athens. He frequently relied on those relationships early in his head coaching career.

If Smart has made a distinct impression in his program, it's with his personality. Otherwise, most of what Georgia does—from establishing the culture to the media rules—comes directly from Smart's time at Alabama.

"Coach Smart learned from Coach Saban," former Georgia outside linebackers coach Kevin Sherrer said. "But Kirby kind of has his way. Coach Saban has his way. They're similar, but [they have] different styles. Coach Smart is younger. He's probably more energetic, relates to the players. But they're very similar. I think Kirby is probably a little more personable."

Glenn Schumann coaches inside linebackers for the Bulldogs and has done so since Smart took the UGA job following the 2015 season. He was also recently promoted to co–defensive coordinator after Dan Lanning accepted the Oregon head coaching job. But previous to that, Schumann was an undergraduate analyst and a graduate assistant under Saban from 2008 to 2015. He's hesitant to compare Smart and

Saban, and that's probably wise considering the egos at play and the remote chance his words could be misunderstood. He wasn't even comfortable discussing the work-life balance and whether it's better at Georgia under Smart than it was at Alabama under Saban.

"I don't like to focus on differences," Schumann said. "There's a lot of similarities in the way day-to-day business is conducted. But they're each their own people. There's a human aspect to this profession. Kirby's different than Nick on a personal level—not better or worse—and so that's the...'difference.' I loved working at Alabama. I loved to work. Both people love to work really hard. So if you love to work, it's a great place to be. I relate well with Nick. I relate well with Kirby. I don't think it's easier to relate to one or the other."

Schumann said he doesn't recall Smart taking the picture of Alabama's recruiting board. He said recruiting is a tough business, and coaches who are successful are expected to get recruits. "I think everybody understands that you do what you have to do to get players," Schumann said. "You try to always be positive and not be negative toward one another. I still talk to Mack Wilson now. I love the kid the same regardless of whether he went to Georgia or Alabama."

Given the level of competition now for elite players, it's bound to lead to some hurt feelings along the way occasionally. That's likely the case for all the programs in the SEC. Perhaps it just feels more personal with Smart because he used to wear crimson and white instead of red and black.

"You don't have to dislike somebody to compete against them," Saban said. "I have a lot of respect for all the guys that worked for me and the guys that did a great job for us when they worked on our staff. I'm happy to see them doing well wherever they go, and when we have to play against them, I'm sure they're doing everything they can to beat us for their team and their players, and we're going to do the same with our players.

"It's not personal. I mean...I don't dislike the guy that I play against. You compete against him and do the best you can, and want to do the best you can for your players on your team."

Alabama and Georgia don't play often, but the frequency has increased since Smart got to Georgia. Saban played Georgia four times with Smart on his staff from 2007 to 2015. And he's played the Bulldogs five times since Smart's been there from 2016 to 2021. But where the programs meet every year is on the recruiting trail, and that's where they'll continue to battle for the best players in the southeast.

"That's probably going to be like that for a long time right now," former UA linebacker Rashaan Evans said. Evans played for Smart under Saban. "I think it's very ironic. It's kind of like it was supposed to happen like this. Kirby was one of those types of guys that I felt like if he were able to ever get a head coaching job, he would be great at it. Same way I feel about [Jeremy] Pruitt. They're great defensive scheme guys. They're very aggressive in their play calling. They're very smart as far as [putting] guys in the right place to be successful. I think that's the reason why Kirby is having so much success, and I think Coach Pruitt will have the same thing. I mean, that's the usual. Kirby does a great job of recruiting. He's always been like that, so I think now it's going to be a triangle. You got Coach Pruitt, Kirby, and Coach Saban. They're probably going to be the top coaches in the SEC. So I'm looking forward to [seeing] how that plays out."

Smart's recruiting prowess has been lethal at Georgia. The 2018 UGA recruiting class halted Alabama's run of No. 1–ranked recruiting classes. It's also one of the greatest classes signed of all time. That signaled that the battle for the top

SEC program would be contested between Saban and Smart, Alabama and Georgia.

When he took the Georgia job, Smart not only hired Schumann and nabbed UA defensive backs coach Mel Tucker to be his defensive coordinator, but the headline-grabbing move was a shocker: He took Scott Cochran, Alabama's longtime strength and conditioning coach. That move was seen as an act of war, further escalating the tensions between the two programs.

Cochran had been with Nick Saban at Alabama since the beginning in 2007. He and head athletic trainer Jeff Allen were the only original staff members remaining after Burton Burns left the program to coach running backs for the New York Giants. Allen is now the lone man standing.

"We appreciate Scott's contribution to our organization over the last 13 years," Saban said in a statement released by Alabama at the time of Cochran's departure. "We can't thank him enough for his service and dedication to our program, and his commitment to our players. He is taking his career in a new direction, and we wish Scott, Cissy, and the kids the best. As we do with every position that opens here, we will go out and hire the best person to lead our strength and conditioning program and help our players maximize the resources available in our new sports science facility."

It wasn't a secret that Cochran had begun reading his own headlines and wanted to advance his career. He wanted to move to an on-the-field coaching position. He'd rebuffed an opportunity to join Smart originally when Smart first took the Georgia head coaching job. And after Ole Miss hired Lane Kiffin in December, the Rebels' new head coach had expressed interest in making Cochran an on-the-field coach. Cochran was considering his options for moving his career forward.

And perhaps rightfully so. It should be noted that Cochran isn't your everyday, run-of-the-mill strength and conditioning coach. At Alabama he famously described his role as taking Bentleys (the players Saban brought into the program) and putting rims on them. In other words, he gets players ready to play in the uber-physical SEC. He brings so much more, though: Players grow under his tutelage, sure, and it's evidenced by the before-and-after images he tweets out, but he also counsels them. He's the guy they turn to when they have a problem with their head coach or position coach. Problems at home or with a girlfriend? Go to Cochran.

He had become such a mainstay of Alabama's program that he was one of the only coaches Saban allowed to talk to the media. He had done interviews with HBO and ESPN. He had even starred in a bank commercial alongside Saban. The school featured him on the Jumbotron during games with his patented "Yeah! Yeah! Yeah!" scream. Cochran used his position to 1) become synonymous with Alabama football, 2) make himself a wealthy man (he made $610,000 before bonus in 2019), and 3) eventually transition to the job he wanted as an on-the-field coach.

Cochran had overestimated his value to Saban. Saban thought he was valuable, sure, but not enough to promote him to a position he didn't think he was ready for. Saban could have easily moved some pieces around the chessboard to make room for Cochran on the field, but he didn't. And that hurt Cochran's feelings.

The desire for upward mobility had been there for a while. Cochran viewed himself as making the move toward coaching. And he did.

For Smart and the Bulldogs, this was as outside-the-box a hire as one could imagine, and a risky one given Cochran's lack of on-field coaching experience. The move caught even many around the program by surprise, as the thinking had become that the job would go to former Southern Miss offensive coordinator Buster Faulkner. Smart instead decided to make a very unexpected move.

No offense to Cochran's X's and O's ability, but he'd mainly been viewed as the motivator for Alabama's football program—the guy on the sideline with his hands up in the air all game long. But he and Smart shared a friendship, and it served as a public relations win for Smart and Georgia to hire Cochran, especially because it came at Alabama's expense. At the time Georgia was recruiting slightly better than Alabama, and then it took one of the Crimson Tide's most important coaches. It was viewed as a major coup.

Saban answered by going an entirely different direction and embracing science in technology by hiring Dr. Matt Rhea and David Ballou to run Alabama's brand-new Sports Science Center. The program had had enough of the self-promotion and the cult of personality with Cochran. They went—forgive the expression—full-on nerd with Rhea and Ballou, who focused more on movement and keeping players fresh and healthy so they could perform their best late in the season.

It was just the latest battle between Saban and Smart. Every time the two programs meet while led by these two particular men, the discussion will always come back to their relationship and their time spent together.

And they'll also meet each other on the recruiting trail each and every season. Saban is going to continue to get the best, and Smart will do the same. The 247Sports.com composite rankings had their respective classes ranked second and third. The more things change, the more they stay the same. Both will always be elite recruiters. And if that means one has to use whatever advantage he has to pull a player from the other, that's what will happen. Smart is going to continue to do what he has to do to get players, and he says Alabama will do the same.

"The cutthroat part is more for media attention," Smart said. "Maybe you feel that way in recruiting or you feel that way to beat somebody. Yeah, you want to win the game for your players and your program, but I mean it's not personal for me and [Alabama's] staff. I have a lot of friends on their staff. I respect their staff. It's not really cutthroat to me. The competitive nature is to go win, but outside of that, they're good people."

4

Burton Burns

You know the Burton Burns who coached double-digit running backs from the University of Alabama practice fields off Hackberry Lane to various NFL squads. You're familiar with the Burton Burns who honed the first Heisman Trophy winners in the program's history and had a third represent in New York City as a finalist. You know the guy who received a minute-long thank-you from Derrick Henry during his 2015 Heisman acceptance speech. You may even know the Burton Burns who turned down overtures and pleas from a sitting Louisiana governor to break the color barrier and become LSU's first African American player in the 1970s only to forge his own path at Nebraska. Or you may have heard that he is the son of a World War II United States Marine Corps veteran awarded the Congressional Gold Medal. But you don't *really* know Burkie, which is what his family and friends call him.

Burns was one of Nick Saban's initial hires when he came to Tuscaloosa and the University of Alabama all those years ago. And Burns stayed loyal to Saban too, even through multiple surgeries to his lower body to keep him upright. He only left in 2020 when an opportunity to coach running backs with the New York Giants presented itself—working in New York and coaching Saquon Barkley.

Burns is remembered fondly in Tuscaloosa, where he coached two Heisman Trophy winners and taught his players about the ins and outs of playing the position at an elite level. Along the way he taught them about loyalty, love, and family too. The search to find a soul who would speak an ill word about Burns would be in vain. Former players remain rigidly loyal to their coach. Ask Derrick Henry or Mark Ingram or Kenyan Drake about what they think about Burkie. You'll have to sit down, because you'll be there a while.

There is the easily identifiable excellence from Burns the coach. Crimson Tide running backs ran for nearly 18 miles under Burns's direction, beginning in 2007—a total of 31,636 yards. Nearly all of his starters have been drafted into the NFL. One of those star pupils, Henry, eclipsed the 2,000-yard mark in the NFL, a high water mark in that league.

If you ever found yourself on an Alabama practice field during his time there, you'd undoubtedly be fascinated by the running backs. No, not by their sheer size or the number of great players you'd spot—although that in its own right was a testament to Burns's eye for talent and recruiting ability—but in how hard he pushed them.

Mark Ingram, UA's first Heisman Trophy winner, arrived in Tuscaloosa from Flint, Michigan, a long way from home and with a lot to learn. "He expected you to know defenses, learn defenses, know fronts, learn how to tell where pressure was coming from, all that," Ingram said. "How to be violent with your cuts, one-step cuts. He was just on you consistently."

You couldn't play for the former Nebraska fullback (1971–75) without a firm understanding of the fundamentals: mastery over footwork, how to press the hole, how to properly carry the ball, how to block, and the importance of a sharp cut upfield, for instance. And if you failed to execute those things, he could dress you down. Yes, the grandfatherly, sweet man could bring you to tears.

Those qualities of demanding perfection and not settling for anything less are things he learned playing for legendary New Orleans high school football coach Otis Washington at St. Augustine. Washington coached at the school for 11 years, from 1969 to 1979, and lost a total of only 17 games. Burns took those lessons with him to Nebraska.

"Burton would knock your teeth out," former Cornhuskers running back teammate Tony Davis said. "Burton played like he coaches. He's a technician, and he's a teacher, and he does these things right. He's got that rare combination of the ability to teach attitude as well as technique. He's just so damn good. He was like that as a player. So this stuff that [he did at Alabama] doesn't surprise me."

After Nebraska, Burns returned home to New Orleans and took a job working for Washington at Saint Augustine in 1975. "I hired him sight unseen," Washington said. When Washington went to Southern University, Burns joined his staff in 1981. From day one he was always a running backs coach, and from day one he demanded a certain style of play. As a player, he tried to run over you; he coached the same way.

That trademark toughness was his calling card, and it carried over to his players. Alabama runners weren't exactly known as scatbacks picking their way at the edges of defenses during his time. Their reputation was that of physical downhill runners. Directly or indirectly, that was reinforced every day with Burns at practice. It was an extension of their coach.

"Burkie is a guy who is not going to let anybody outwork him," his brother Ronnie Burns said back when Burns was still at UA. "He's going to teach the fundamentals. He's going to make sure those guys do the drills to perfection and make sure they know why they're doing those drills. When he recruits a player, he's looking for a certain mentality of player. Obviously they're talented, but they have to have that mental edge to them too: 'We don't give up. We don't quit. We follow all the way through.' And I think he teaches that in his drills. He gets fired up when he's coaching."

That tenacity in his coaching style wasn't just something he preached. He lived it. It was the way he played—the only way he knew how to. "I will tell you that of the 10 or 11 running backs you'd pair up against and go against each other [back at Nebraska], I always tried to avoid Burton because he would just knock your...teeth out," Davis said. "There was no ease-up. It was always you just got drilled. With Burton he was 5'10", 5'11", 230 pounds, and he could run and he had power. He had that snap. When he arrived to the pile, the...pile exploded."

With his players at Alabama, Burns had the ability to see beyond what they wanted and give them what they *needed*. Sometimes that involved intentionally angering them or manufacturing something to motivate them. He quickly figured out what got under a player's skin and used it to extract the best from them. "I think he understands the hot buttons of these kids," Ronnie Burns said. "That's a talent all in its own—to understand what motivates you, what motivates me. He knows how to press those buttons."

That applied to Derrick Henry, a notoriously driven player who was known for being the hardest worker on the team and a sort of self-starter. You've likely seen the videos of Henry's off-season workouts, the chains on his back as he does pushups. His level of work ethic was legendary, but even he was the subject of Burkie's motivational ploys. "He would say things just to get you motivated, things he knew you were thinking about and wanted to get better at," Henry said. "He was always listening to you to make sure he constantly stayed on you just so he did his job to help you get better and make sure you were working hard. That's the biggest thing for me is he would nag me on things I needed to get better at, and he made sure they stayed in your mind."

With Ingram, a player who welcomed truthful feedback, Burns knew there was no out-of-bounds. "I didn't mind criticism or him being rough on me," Ingram said. "He would push me and be on me. If there [were times when] I thought I was practicing good and he thought I was slacking off, he'd let me know. Then I'd come to practice ready the next day. [He'd] lift you up and [he'd] bring you down. If you needed encouragement, he'd encourage you. He knew when to be tough on you and to make you get right. That's why he's my favorite coach who I've ever played for."

Burns is a tough and unrelenting taskmaster, but he's also a big softie—a loving father of four and grandfather of two who cares for his players old and new alike, like they are a part of his own family. It is in those competing ideals where one can find the real Burns. Call it the duality of Burkie.

There is the side of the man few see—a man so completely heartbroken by the death of a former player, Altee Tenpenny, that for a time after the young man's passing, no running back was allowed to sit in his seat in the meeting room. His players see that side; they saw it on October 20, 2015—the day Tenpenny died in a one-car accident in Mississippi. It hit Burns and the team hard.

Behind the scenes Burns had been working with Tenpenny since the North Little Rock, Arkansas, native arrived on campus. At first he worked developing the player. More and more, though, it became about counseling the person, trying to keep him at Alabama despite some setbacks. After it became apparent things weren't going to work out for Tenpenny in Tuscaloosa, Burns made phone calls to other programs to make sure he had a landing spot. Then came the call that Tenpenny, just 20 years old, was gone.

Those in Burkie's inner circle say he was devastated. One person close to Burns said, "It caused him to think deep about how much more he could have done to help him. He did everything in his power, but he was sad because, in the end, it didn't save him."

When the news broke, Burns called a meeting with his running backs. He wanted them to be together, to be a family in that moment. "He really was heartbroken," Henry said. "When Altee passed, he talked to us and told us just to remember the good times with Altee and how he was. That's what Altee would want us to remember him as…. You could sense that he always loved Altee."

That love and sense of family comes from within for Burkie. He comes from an extraordinarily close family. His father, Winston Burns, was a junior varsity and high school football coach in his day under whom the legendary Otis Washington did his student teaching.

The Burnses are beloved in their native New Orleans. They are beloved in Tuscaloosa. It seems that anyone who comes in contact with the Burns family, and especially Burton and his wife of more than 40 years, Connie, can't help but love them. "It's trite, and maybe an oversimplification, but they're just good," New Orleans media member and area sports historian Ro Brown said. "You just come away from them knowing that they're just so good. And I'm talking as a collective. [They're] just quality people. They treat people the right way."

Recently Tony Davis was instrumental in presenting his friend Burkie with the Alumni of Excellence Award awarded by the Nebraska Greats Foundation. It was the first time the award had been given.

Alabama and LSU are bitter rivals. You're either crimson and white or you're purple and gold. There's no straddling the fence. But Burton courts such love, even those wearing purple and gold rooted for the legendary Alabama coach. "Whether you're an LSU fan or not, people respect him and they like him because he's good," Brown said. "They know he [coached] at Alabama. I wished he was at LSU."

Ingram can still hear his old coach when he fumbles or messes up during a drill with the New Orleans Saints. He knows that demand for excellence comes from a place of love. "All the goals you have for yourself, he wants those and more for you," Ingram said. "He's just a special guy and a special person and a special coach all in one.

"His family loves you. His wife, Mrs. Connie, she's amazing. They take you in. I was far, far away from home when I went to Alabama, and they embraced me and made me feel at home. They're family still to this day."

5

Bryant and Saban: More Similar Than Different

SPEND ENOUGH TIME IN A COTTON FIELD ROOTING AROUND in the soil, and it's as if you can't get rid of the dirt. The dust settles in the crevices of your hands, the grime creeps under your fingernails, and a film sort of coats your lungs. Paul W. "Bear" Bryant was reared in that dirt as part of a family of sharecroppers in Moro Bottom, Arkansas.

Nick Saban grew up in a coal-mining community in Idamay, West Virginia, the son of a gas station owner. He never spent time in the earth the way those around him must have, but as an attendant at his father's station, he saw the black smeared faces of men who did, bone-weary and exhausted after another shift in the mines.

Both Bryant and Saban chose to carve roads that assured they'd never have to return to the dirt of their youth, driven to make their paths in the world differently—driven to the emerald green fields they patrolled so expertly in their professional lives. Kind of ironic that both, so stridently driven to escape the dirt, found their lives' calling teaching a game born in it.

When you take the chisel to the granite to carve out the game's coaching Mount Rushmore, two faces are sure to be sculpted, and both plied their trade at Alabama. The other two spots are up for debate and could just as easily be coaches from another singular school, Notre Dame: Knute Rockne and Frank Leahy. But Bryant and Saban are so secure in their spots in the game's lore, it's safe to put hammer to chisel. They are the two greatest college football coaches of all time. That they both wound their way to Alabama, where both had the most success of their respective careers—is either one big coincidence or speaks to what can be done there. Either way, Alabama employed the two greatest to ever do it.

This is how two men—strangers to one another—found greatness in Tuscaloosa, Alabama, of all places. This is about championships, transformation, and legacy. This is the story of Bryant, Saban, and Alabama, and how they all came together to create the best college football coaching legacy of all time.

Combined they claim 13 national championships and 24 SEC championships. To put that into context, that's 11 more conference titles than the second-place programs in the league claim (Georgia and Tennessee each have 13 SEC championships). That's also more national titles than any other school in the country can claim.

Bryant retired as the game's winningest coach. Saban will never approach Bryant's 323 collegiate wins, but the rate at which Saban is clicking off national titles is also unmatched.

Saban's six national championships at Alabama in 12 years has never been achieved before in the history of college football. In a game set up for parity, it's unlikely it will ever be equaled.

Ivan Maisel is a college football reporter and historian. Having grown up in Mobile, Alabama, Maisel knows the ins and outs of Crimson Tide football and the eras in which both Bryant and Saban competed. Prior to Saban's arrival in Tuscaloosa in 2007, no active coach in the country was closer than four national championships away from equaling Bryant. Since then, Saban has won six to surpass him.

"I'm surprised anybody tied Bryant," Maisel said. "It was one of those records that I think—I won't say everyone but most of us—thought was inviolate. And to see a coach do it and do it in such a short amount of time is really remarkable."

It's not just that Saban has done what most consider nearly impossible, it's that he has done so in such a short span. Bryant won 6 national titles in 25 seasons at Alabama. Saban won 6 in his 15 seasons at UA to date. In that regard, Saban is probably most similar to John McKay at the University of Southern California, who won 4 national titles in 16 seasons from 1960 to 1975. To put that into context, Saban is averaging a national title every 2.5 seasons compared to McKay's 1 every 4 seasons.

Bryant and Saban each arrived at Alabama with three previous college head coaching jobs on their résumés. Bryant spent one season (1945) at Maryland, eight (1946–53) at Kentucky, and four (1954–57) at Texas A&M. Saban got his first head coaching opportunity at Toledo, where he spent one season (1990), then spent five seasons (1995–99) at Michigan State, and five (2000–04) at LSU.

During their respective tenures at Alabama, Bryant compiled a 232–46–9 record and Saban has a 183–25 mark. Bryant went 12–10–2 in bowl games while Saban has gone

15–6 (including the College Football Playoff). Bryant's Alabama teams spent 29 weeks ranked as the No. 1 team in the country and compiled a record of 26–4 as the top-ranked team. Saban's UA squads have spent 106 weeks, or 43 percent of his tenure in Tuscaloosa, at No. 1. As a program, Alabama's 137 weeks at No. 1 is best in the country ahead of second-place Ohio State (105 weeks).

Bryant welcomed the opportunity to learn from other greats. It was in his seminal autobiography, *Bear: The Hard Life and Good Times of Alabama's Coach Bryant*, that Bryant expressed his most regular phone conversations were with Darrell Royal, McKay, Bobby Dodd, and Bud Wilkinson. So it's not a stretch to think he would have tried to cozy up to Saban.

"I bet they would've been friends," Maisel said. "McKay was a good friend of his, Darrell Royal was a close friend of his. I don't think that's an accident. Those guys respected one another and enjoyed each other's company and respected what they were able to achieve. They could talk shop and compare notes. The great anecdote about Bryant signing John Mitchell to play began because it was the off-season and he was out drinking with McKay. I don't know how buddy-buddy Saban is with any other coach, but I think he would've gotten along with Bryant and respected him. I think they would've gotten along just fine."

Likewise, Saban has spent time with different coaches in each off-season (Bob Stoops, Gary Patterson, Tom Herman, Jason Garrett), always learning, always trying to get better.

What makes both men—who don't appear to have a lot in common outside the game of football—alike in greatness is that neither shied away from change. They made their respective ways to the top one way, and they stayed on top by adjusting. In fact, perhaps it is in their ability to adapt that the men are *most* similar. Bryant's adaptation is more pronounced simply because he coached in three distinct eras of college football: two-way players, specialty players, and integration.

The anecdote Maisel referenced provides a snapshot of a couple signature moments in Bryant's career. When he visited with McKay in a hotel that Sunday afternoon in Houston in the winter of 1970, Bryant had already signed his first Black player—Wilbur Jackson—to integrate his program. Alabama was coming off back-to-back six-win seasons in 1969 and '70, and Bryant was at a crossroads in his career: He wasn't winning at the rate he had throughout most of the 1960s, and he was tackling the integration of his football team head-on during a time when the subject was highly contentious in the Deep South.

Bryant sat with McKay and learned of a player, John Mitchell, who was originally from Mobile and who was playing at East Arizona State, a junior college. Bryant quietly excused himself, found a telephone, and called back to Tuscaloosa to get someone to Mobile immediately to recruit Mitchell, an African American defensive lineman. Mitchell ultimately chose the Crimson Tide and became the first Black player to play a down of football for UA. He was the first Alabama starter, the first Black captain, the first Black UA All-American, and eventually the program's first Black assistant coach.

Mitchell's first game just so happened to occur on the same night Bryant unveiled his new wishbone offense, the one that took USC by such surprise and allowed Alabama to begin the season with a 17–10 victory over the No. 5–ranked Trojans in Los Angeles. Bryant made the radical change in his program by sending two of his assistants, Mal Moore and Jimmy Sharpe, to Austin, Texas, to learn the offensive system from Darrell Royal, who had begun running the wishbone in 1968 at the University of Texas. It was only one game, but in two distinctly different ways—integration and the debut of the wishbone—it reshaped the Alabama program and Bryant's legacy, setting the stage for the dominant 1970s decade that was to come.

Saban also dealt with alteration. First it was in what is known as the Saban Rule, which the NCAA instituted to restrict college head coaches from doing on-the-road evaluations of high school players during the spring—in short, to combat Saban's rock-star status and the massive publicity he was generating with every stop to visit a prospect at a high school. To deal with that, Saban became one of the first coaches, if not the first, to talk to recruits via Skype during the spring.

When the game evolved beginning around 2012–13 to incorporate the hurry-up, no-huddle offense, Saban's big, sometimes lumbering defense was caught flat-footed. So he changed his philosophy in recruiting to incorporate more athletic, sometimes smaller, defensive linemen and quicker linebackers. The result? Two of his linebackers—C. J. Mosley and Reuben Foster—won the Butkus Award as the best at their position in the country in their respective seasons. While it's true that Mosley was already on the team before Saban changed his recruiting model, his skill set was perfect for the new-look UA defender. And Alabama won three national championships since then: in 2015, 2017, and 2020.

"It's a different thing, but I think our program here is unquestionably the top program in the country and has been, and [Saban] has maintained it and worked hard to keep it," said Bryant's son, Paul Bryant Jr. "We had that in the '60s and '70s, but it was different with a poll situation rather than a playoff like we have now.

"Our players were more from Alabama then—we had them from all over the country but primarily from Alabama—and I think they came to win championships. Now, from what I read, I think a lot of them come because they want to play in the NFL. It was a little bit different dynamic back then.

"They both had a deal built around defense and the kicking game and winning at the line of scrimmage and playing a physical game of football. Everybody talks about the offenses [being different], but I think that's the similarity."

Saban was initially against the changes he was seeing in the game, famously asking, "Is this what we want football to be?" But he came to fully embrace them, recruiting dual-threat quarterbacks and bringing in Lane Kiffin as his offensive coordinator to install hurry-up and spread tendencies in his own offense. Kiffin helped Alabama accumulate three straight SEC championships, three straight SEC Offensive Player of the Year awards, a Heisman Trophy winner, and a Heisman Trophy finalist.

Both Bryant and Saban recognized that they had to evolve to keep winning. "It was more dire with Bryant," Maisel said. "Saban never got down to going 6–5–1, he never had consecutive six-win seasons. I think it speaks to an understanding that the game is constantly changing and you have to constantly adjust. I think Saban gets more points in that regard because he recognized it more quickly. Bryant in the late 1960s—as he later said, he was distracted and he had kind of taken his eye off the ball. Once he fixed it, it turned around pretty fast. Saban never let it get that bad."

Bryant might be remembered differently without the 1970s, which included an astounding eight SEC championships and three national titles. He'd still be a legend, no doubt, but had he accepted an offer from the Miami Dolphins to become head coach in the winter of 1969, his legacy would be different. He seriously considered the chance to coach the National Football

League team, but when he told Alabama officials of the decision he was weighing, he just couldn't pull the trigger. "That night I told [Dolphins owner] Joe Robbie I'd take the job but that I'd have to get the approval of my people first," Bryant wrote in his biography. "And when it came down to the nut-cutting, I couldn't do it."

"I think it was worth his consideration, and I think he gave it an awful lot of thought," said John Underwood, who coauthored Bryant's biography. "I think something happened with him and Alabama too, in regards to compensation and all the effort. He made the wise choice, of course. He would not have hesitated to go if he thought that was the best thing all around. I think Miami would've benefited greatly."

Coincidentally, it was with the same Dolphins that Saban's trajectory altered. He departed LSU for Miami after five successful seasons that included a national title (2003) and two SEC championships (2001 and 2003). Many felt he had the Tigers on the verge of a historical run in Baton Rouge. During his two seasons in Miami, Saban realized he had made a mistake and that he and his wife, Terry, enjoyed the college game and the influence they could have on student-athletes.

Saban received overtures from Alabama following their 2006 season, but he wanted to live up to his word and contract with then–Dolphins owner Wayne Huizenga. But Mal Moore, UA's athletics director at the time, wouldn't take no for an answer. After infamously saying, "I'm not going to be the Alabama coach," Saban relented and boarded a plane bound for Tuscaloosa to start his momentous run.

Bryant used his influence in a positive way at Alabama. The Bryant Scholarship was established in the 1970s and benefits sons and daughters of men who played for Bryant during his 25 years as the UA coach. The total dollar amount of the scholarships donated in Bryant's name has surpassed the money the legendary coach made in salary as UA's coach. To date, nearly 1,000 students have been recipients, including Charley and Trey Waldrep, the sons of Kent Waldrep, a running back for TCU who suffered paralysis while being tackled by an Alabama defender in 1974. When his sons reached college age, Moore extended the Bryant Scholarships to them. "The man behind the legend is the one that is truly near and dear to our hearts and really bonded us with not only the University of Alabama but the people in Alabama, because they really had an impact on my dad," Trey Waldrep said.

Bryant also did untold good for people across the state, and some stories of his largesse have emerged. Richmond Flowers Jr. was a standout athlete at Sidney Lanier High School in Montgomery. His father was the state's attorney general from 1963 to 1967, during the height of the civil rights era. Flowers Jr. chose to go to Tennessee to play football and run track despite holding an offer from Bryant. After his playing days were over, he wanted to attend law school but was denied admission at Tennessee. He went to Bryant to ask for a favor, and the coach intervened. Flowers was admitted to the UA law school.

In late November 1968 Bryant showed a sensitive side not everyone got to see. One of his favorite former players, Pat Trammell, phoned to tell his coach that he had cancer. Bryant accompanied him to New York City for treatment. The cancer eventually won and Trammell passed. Bryant described Trammell's passing as "the saddest day of my life." The school now honors the late quarterback with an award given annually in his name to the Alabama football player who demonstrates the qualities of integrity, character, importance of academics, and inspirational leadership.

Bryant's legacy remains as strongly intact in Tuscaloosa today as was in 1983 when he passed. You'll spot Bryant Coca-Cola bottles on mantels in homes across the state. The majority of UA's athletic facilities sit off Bryant Drive. Across the street, you'll find the Bryant Museum. Bryant remains royalty.

Saban has his philanthropic ways too, mainly through his Nick's Kids Foundation, which he runs with his wife, Terry. Through the charity, the Sabans have built 18 Habitat for Humanity homes. The charity has distributed more than $6 million to state organizations. The couple has also given a $1 million donation to the First Generation Scholarships Program at the University of Alabama.

Saban also exhibits under-the-radar kindnesses. When offensive tackle Aaron Douglas passed away from an accidental drug overdose in the spring of 2011, Saban kept his family close to the team. After the Crimson Tide won the national championship in the ensuing season, the coach awarded the family the championship ring to which Douglas would have been entitled had he been around to play.

Both coaches have busts at the Mal Moore Building and statues along the Walk of Champions outside Bryant-Denny Stadium. No building or street is currently named for Saban, but there have been preliminary talks to address the issue in some capacity at an undetermined future date.

The thing about genius is that it's not intimidated by greatness in others. The reasons are probably better argued by psychologists than journalists, but essentially this is due to the comfort genius enjoys in its security of its place. That is, it recognizes its brilliance and isn't cowed by others who achieve at a high level. The lion doesn't concern itself with the opinions of sheep. So after the 2017 national championship, when Saban tied Bryant's record of six national championships, those who knew Bryant said he would've been overjoyed. It was the same after the 2020 title that surpassed Bryant. It's reasonable to assume Bryant might have made the first congratulatory phone call to Saban. Bryant never felt insecure in the presence of the game's greats. Quite the opposite, actually; he enjoyed close friendships with USC's John McKay and Texas's Darrell Royal and frequently spoke to Georgia Tech's Bobby Dodd and Oklahoma's Bud Wilkinson—all men who were accomplished peers in his day.

In other words, Bryant never shrank in the shadow of greatness cast by others in his business. He embraced that greatness. And Saban is the same way: Even though he is now on top in terms of national championships, he still considers Bryant the best ever to do it. "I think Coach Bryant is sort of in a class of his own in terms of what he was able to accomplish, what his record is, the longevity that he had, and the tradition he established," Saban said. "If it wasn't for Coach Bryant, we would never be able to do what we did."

Each man defined his respective era. Each faced threats to his dominion and overcame them. Each dealt with changes to the game in different ways while persevering and winning. Bryant navigated the social and athletic adjustments of the integration of southern football in a tumultuous era not too far removed from fire hoses and attack dogs. Saban is competing in an age of limited scholarships that is fraught with its own societal challenges, including the advent of social media giving players their own platforms to voice opinions. Both men are considered masters at their use of the media both locally and nationally, each using the media to forge the Alabama program's image, albeit in his own way.

Saban, a man with a well-established contempt for comparisons, may well need to come to terms with his curriculum vitae being juxtaposed with Bryant's from now until he decides to place his straw hat on the rack for the final time.

It's not entirely fair to ask if Saban is encroaching upon Bryant's legacy, but there are certainly conversations being held about which coach is greater. That too is probably an uneven debate given how they coached during different eras. Saban always expresses his opinion when the subject is broached. "I think Coach Bryant is probably the best coach of all time because of the longevity of his tenure as a coach and the way he changed," Saban said. "I mean, he won championships running the wishbone. He won them with Joe Namath dropping back throwing when people never, ever did it. I just think that, for his time, he impacted the game and had more success than anybody ever could."

And again, those who knew Bryant say he would been one of Saban's biggest fans. "I think 'Bear' Bryant...would've been delighted that somebody with not just the smarts but the understanding of what football's all about and why it's such a great sport [toppled his record]," John Underwood said. "Because he didn't mind expressing his opinion. I don't have any doubt that Bryant would have applauded. He didn't believe in records going unbroken forever. He believed that records were to be broken. I mean, because he certainly broke a few."

It's unlikely anyone, including Saban, will approach the veneration Bryant holds. Bryant played at Alabama, famously played with a broken leg against Tennessee, embraced Alabama's two great rivalries (Auburn and Tennessee), and spent 25 years as the coach of the Crimson Tide. And he did so at a time in the state's history when there wasn't much to be proud of nationally. In that regard, no one will ever touch how beloved he is.

That's not a slight to Saban, who has brought pride and respect back to a program that had spent the better part of a decade wandering in the wilderness before he began restoring it in 2007. It's just that once you've loved deeply for so long, can you really love that deeply in the same way again? "It's a good question," Maisel said. "I don't know. Bryant was loved in a way that I'm not sure Saban is loved. People were so emotionally attached to Bryant. I'm not sure. I don't think the emotional attachment to Saban is quite as strong. But that's Nick's personality. He's an introvert in a lot of ways. And Bryant was a ham. He loved attention; he loved to be around people. Nick's not that way.... I know [people will] miss [Saban, and] when his run of success ends, they're going to expect the next guy to do the same, and we've all seen the song and dance in the 1980s and '90s, and this one's going to be worse—this amount of success is greater and more concentrated. The withdrawal from that is going to be ugly."

Saban's list of accolades and achievements is long and varied. He's won the Paul "Bear" Bryant Coach of the Year Award twice. But Bryant's name still rings out across campus. None of what Saban accomplishes will subtract from the Bryant legacy. He's been gone 39 years, and it's still going strong.

How will these men be remembered? The easy answer is, "As winners." The more complex question—which will cause debate, as does any subjective topic—is which coach will be known as the greatest of all time? No one can say, but the two coaches seemingly emphasized opposite criteria for this metric.

"For me, it's more about the relationships with people—treating people the right way and having compassion for other people," Saban said. "Appreciating the people who have been good friends. I think those are the things that mean the most to me. What the people closest to me say in terms of the kind of person you were and the kind of life you lived. It's not really about how many games you win, or [if] you [won] the most games or…the most championships or [if you] were…the best coach. It's really about how the people that know you well really think about what kind of person you were and what…you really contribute[d] to them."

Bryant expressed a desire to be recalled for what he did best. "When people ask me what…I want to be remembered for, I have one answer," Bryant once said. "I want the people to remember me as a winner, 'cause I ain't never been nothing but a winner."

Just outside the north end of Bryant-Denny Stadium, a bronze statue of each man stands. The years of each man's national championships are carved just behind their likenesses. Bryant's read: 1961, 1964, 1965, 1973, 1978, and 1979. Saban's latest entry was carved out at the latest national championship celebration, revealing a fresh 2020. The two men stand facing the same direction, always looking ahead.

PART 2

THE LEGENDS

6

Julio Jones

How do you reconcile what Julio Jones symbolized for a program early in its development and the actual, relatively humble, stats he compiled? Make no mistake, Jones was the best individual player on every Alabama team he competed on from 2008 to 2010, and his stats still speak for themselves, but he came along at a time when the Crimson Tide offense wasn't as explosive and efficient as it is now, nor did he play with the caliber of quarterbacks that have populated more recent UA rosters. He doesn't rank in the top five for career receiving yards, and Jameson Williams had as many receiving touchdowns in one season as Jones did in three (15). It was a different era of UA football when Jones was there, but his importance to what Saban built is immense.

Ask any Crimson Tide fan who the most important recruit Nick Saban ever landed at Alabama is, and the majority will likely tell you Julio Jones. Usually it takes time for the mythology of a player to build to Hercules-like status. It was never that way with No. 8, Jones. He was a walking myth, a legend in his own time. He remains so in Crimson Tide lore.

He's remembered for what he did in his time, in the infancy of the Alabama dynasty, but it's also easy to lose yourself in a daydream of what could have been had he played on the modern UA offenses. During his time, the team ran the ball and played elite defense. Since then the Alabama program has become known for producing elite passing games; it has morphed into a program that has produced six of the last eight SEC Offensive Player of the Year winners, all but one of them either a wide receiver or quarterback:

2014: Amari Cooper, wide receiver

2015: Derrick Henry, running back

2016: Jalen Hurts, quarterback

2018: Tua Tagovailoa, quarterback

2020: DeVonta Smith, wide receiver

2021: Bryce Young, quarterback

So what would Jones have looked like in a current Crimson Tide offense? One can only dream. "It'd be sick," former assistant coach Lance Thompson said. Thompson, who recruited the Mobile area for Saban during his tenure there, personally handled Jones's recruitment and got to know him and his mom, Queen, quite well. "There wouldn't be anybody like him. If he had played with this guy Bryce Young—. Julio played with John Parker [Wilson] and [Greg] McElroy, and I like them both, but they're both possession guys. They're not pro-style quarterbacks. If he had played with Mac Jones—as well as he throws the long ball—shit, he might have had 2,000 yards in a single season."

Thompson's probably not far off. Amari Cooper had 1,727 yards in 2014, and DeVonta Smith, the program's career leading receiver in nearly every category, had 1,856 in his Heisman Trophy year, 2020. So the thought of Jones, a physical freak, topping 2,000 yards isn't that crazy.

But Jones played when he played in that specific era of Crimson Tide football and put up great numbers for his day in that offense. It was that offense, though, that had many questioning whether or not Alabama was the place for him. There were other programs, teams such as Oklahoma, that featured the passing offense in their systems. Many thought it was Oklahoma where he'd land. It might have been had Saban not taken over and had Thompson not been responsible for recruiting him.

You have to understand, Jones was a big deal even early on at his alma mater Foley High School in Foley, Alabama. Thompson remembered a time at a jamboree game when he sat with Alabama legend and Pro Football Hall of Fame and College Football Hall of Fame member Ozzie Newsome. The two were watching Jones, and it was clear what was in front of them. "We're sitting there telling stories about Ken Stabler, and Julio catches like two balls, and Ozzie looks at me and says, 'This guy's a Hall of Famer,'" Thompson said. "Julio is just a different breed. He looks like an avatar. The guy's a stud."

Thompson spent many hours down on the Alabama Gulf Coast recruiting Jones and other members of that seminal 2008 Crimson Tide recruiting class, guys such as Mark Barron and B. J. Scott. "[Jones is] the one that changed the whole shebang," Thompson said. "And everybody knows that. The whole class with him and Mark Barron, those kids I signed those first two years—those 12 to 14 kids I signed, they really established a whole program. They put it back to Bear Bryant standards, but it was Nick Saban's standards, which was like Bryant's run on steroids."

Thompson spent some of those nights in south Alabama sitting on a porch with Queen or eating with Queen. There was a lot of time spent with Queen. "The first time I met her, she said, 'I've heard about you,'" Thompson said. "And I said, 'I've heard about you too, baby.' So we got to know each other real good. So me and Queen got to be good friends, and we hung out a lot of nights just sitting on her front porch, her drinking her margarita, and just looking at the stars. She's a great lady."

Jones was a must-get for Alabama. He was a program changer, and they knew it. But they had to get there first. Thompson always felt good about the recruitment. Saban, the constant perfectionist who leaves nothing to chance, wasn't so sure. He bombarded Thompson with questions about Julio every other day. "I knew he was coming [to Alabama], but I didn't tell Nick because Nick would bug the shit out of me every day," Thompson said. "He'd ask, 'Are we getting Julio? Are we getting Julio?' And I'd tell him, 'I think so, Coach.' And he said, 'When are you going to know?' And I said, 'He's going to make his signing day decision.' But Julio had told me in December or January that he'd always dreamed of going to Alabama but that Alabama just hadn't recruited him right."

So signing day came around, and most die-hard Alabama fans watched his decision play out live and can still tell you to this day what color sweater he was wearing (it was yellow). In front of his school and televised across the country, Jones said: "I'm going to make my decision by where I feel most comfortable and where I feel like home at. So I'm going to be going to the University of Alabama."

You probably didn't hear much after that because the Foley High School gymnasium erupted into elation. I was watching that announcement from Doug Walker's media relations office inside Coleman Coliseum. We were there for the press conference that would occur later that day, and he graciously invited us in to watch. As we watched the announcement, we all kind of took in the moment and, speaking for myself, you could tell things were changing around Alabama football. There wasn't a guarantee, of course, but things felt different.

Not even Saban knew before the announcement despite Thompson giving his assurances. To this day, it remains Saban's most important recruit, in my opinion. "We already had gotten commitments from three or four receivers, and I was worried, because Julio was coming down to the wire, that he would look at it like, 'Well, you've already got all these receivers. Why would you need me?'" Saban told the *Athletic*. "But he never looked at it that way. He always looked at it like, 'I'm going to choose the school I want to go to and where I have the best chance to be successful, and where I have a chance to compete and play with anybody that's there.' That was never an issue with him.

"But he was kind of quiet, so it was hard to get a feel for him. The unique thing about it all is once you got to know him, you have a great relationship with him. Very easy to talk to. That was the tough thing about recruiting him—you never got much of a feel for him because he didn't say much. After he got here, we developed a relationship that's probably one of the best I've ever had with any player."

Jones has a natural presence because of his frame. He looks like he was specifically built in a lab to play wide receiver. Great height, long arms, and not an ounce of fat on him. So people noticed when he entered a room or encountered him in the weight room or saw him on the practice field.

Barrett Jones was also a part of that recruitment class. He was a part of the ground shifting underneath Alabama football.

They were the new breeds—on board with the fundamental changes Saban was implementing. Some existing members of the football team didn't appreciate that new ways, but it was obvious to everyone: Get on board or get left behind. In that regard, both Joneses helped establish the new way things were going to go.

"Julio is obviously the most special of the group just talent-wise," Barrett Jones said. "He was kind of the headliner of the class, and there was a lot of expectations on him. Sometimes you'd find yourself thinking, *Is this guy really what they're saying he is?* But he was just different from the start. I mean, I never saw him tired. He would always just run and he would win most of the sprints that we had to run, and I remember thinking to myself that he was just never tired. He was always out there running from day one. And physically he looked like a senior.

"It was cool for the rest of the class to see Julio working like that because we were all kind of like, 'OK, we can all make a difference. We can make an immediate impact.' [We realized we didn't] have to wait until we were juniors. But with that [came] some disrespect and a feeling where some of the older guys were kind of mad at the new guys because things were changing. But we thought, *You know, hey, it hasn't been working around here with the way y'all are doing things, so we're going to come in here and be a part of the way this place changes.* They did not like Julio coming in and starting over the seniors. It was a weird transition, but you knew it was coming with Julio."

It was obvious to those inside the program because they saw the talent and the work ethic, but it crystallized within the fan base thanks to a blurry video shot from far away at a scrimmage that fall. That was all it took. On it you see quarterback John Parker Wilson flushed out of the pocket and running to this right when he uncorks a long ball down the right sideline to

Jones, who brings it in and then proceeds to stiff-arm All-American safety Rashad Johnson into the turn on his way to a touchdown. It set message boards on fire. If it wasn't already known before, that moment cemented an unwavering belief that Alabama had a freak on its hands.

It wasn't just that he could run fast or jump high, and he could certainly do those things with ease. It was the physical nature with which he played the game. He was a ferocious and willing blocker. If he got his big hands on a defensive back, you were going backward. He ran through tacklers. It often took more than one tackler to bring him down. And he played when he was nicked up. In other words, he was tough.

No game exemplifies all those things more than the LSU game in Baton Rouge in his freshman season in 2008. He was banged up in that game, but it did not deter him from displaying toughness and producing, and ultimately making the play that everyone remembers. "He's the toughest wide receiver I've ever been around," Thompson said. "The guy played like a linebacker. He intimidated people, man. Remember the catch he made in overtime against LSU? The back-shoulder throw?"

I remember it. It set up the game-winning quarterback sneak by Wilson in overtime. For the game, Jones recorded 7 receptions for 128 yards, including the game's penultimate play.

On the Crimson Tide's first play of overtime after LSU threw an interception on its possession, everyone on the sideline knew who was getting the ball: the freshman. Wilson faked a handoff to Glen Coffee and then threw a perfect back-shoulder spiral to Jones, who grabbed it, stayed in bounds, and dragged LSU cornerback Patrick Peterson to the 1-yard line. The next play Wilson snuck it in for the walk-off win. "Everybody in our organization knew, because Nick had already told us, 'Hey, on the first play of overtime, we're throwing a deep ball to Julio on a back-shoulder throw,'" Thompson said. "And we threw it, he caught it, and we scored and won the game."

With the No. 1 ranking on the line and only needing a field goal to win, Nick Saban trusted a freshman the most. That kind of says it all, doesn't it? He did it again a year later as No. 1 Alabama was down late in the fourth quarter to Auburn in Jordan-Hare Stadium. On the final drive, they leaned on him again and again as the offense positioned itself to score. He had 9 catches for 83 yards on the day. And four of those came on the final drive, two on third down. He was reliable.

The rest is quite literally history. He showed that immense talent the rest of his career, and after three years in Tuscaloosa, it was evident that he was ready for the next challenge. The Atlanta Falcons recognized that talent and traded up in the 2011 NFL Draft to get him with the sixth overall selection, giving up five draft picks to get into position to draft him.

It turns out Newsome might have been right all along. Nothing is guaranteed, but it seems certain that Jones will join Newsome in the Pro Football Hall of Fame. "He's a stud, man," Barrett Jones said. "There's no denying it. I know he's not done yet, but when he's healthy, he's as good as any receiver I've ever seen. He's such a talented guy, but he mixes talent with just hard work. He's the total package. Occasionally you get a guy who's that dude. He's so quiet. He just goes in and works and is a leader and is so physical. He's a monster—a 6'3" monster. Have you seen him without a shirt on? He's a cyborg. So yeah, he was different."

So how do you quantify what Jones meant to Alabama at that moment in time? "What do you mean?" Thompson said. "Julio *was* the program at that point. If we don't get Julio, Alabama's not what it is now. I tell everyone that Julio was the pied piper. When Julio came, they all came. Julio was the fucking standard that Nick wanted to set in terms of work ethic, toughness, maturity, discipline—all that because Alabama was just a house of cards before him and that 2008 class just a bunch of guys that didn't really love ball. And then when Julio shows up on campus, he's the motherfucker that everybody follows. And if they don't follow him, they're not there very long. I mean, like I tell people, yeah, it's cool and sexy to go to Alabama now, but when Julio made the decision to go to Alabama, we were 7–6 and getting beat by ULM and Mississippi State. So that guy was the standard setter.

"He's the toughest kid I've ever been around. A football player who worked his ass off. He's the player others were scared to death of. Listen, man, good players are good players. But great players make good players better. Julio is a great player."

7

Derrick Henry

IT'S EASY TO FORGET NOW THAT HE WEARS THE TITLE OF King Henry and is one of the faces of the NFL, now that he's proved to be one of the biggest weapons in the league. But there was a time—in high school and again in college—when those at the next league openly questioned if Derrick Henry could play running back. I'm not kidding. Those were actual questions some raised.

He'd been the biggest kid on the playground in high school, literally like a grown man playing against the smaller kids. That's how it looked, and the results showed that was actually how it was. But when it was time for him to go to college, those who project such things thought he'd be a linebacker. But Henry never saw himself as a linebacker because he was a running back. He was a great running back. But his size made some think he'd grow out of running back at the next level and that his future lay on the defensive side of the ball. But he never did outgrow it. Oh, he grew, but instead of growing out of the position, he simply ran over anyone who got in his way. He ran all the way to the program's second Heisman Trophy during a historic season in 2015 that saw him rush for 2,219 yards and 28 touchdowns. He still holds those records for the SEC, though Najee Harris came close to his single-season rushing touchdown mark in 2020 with 26.

Derrick Henry has been a big deal for a long time, literally and figuratively. He was the big man having a big season and leading nearly all season long during his Heisman run. He was the guy who was constantly besieged by autograph seekers and those wanting a picture. He's been a big fish in a small pond since he was a freshman at Yulee High School, a school in a small town in northeast Florida with a population of just more than 10,000, where he rushed for nearly 2,500 yards as a 15-year-old. As a senior—a season in which he once rushed for 510 yards in a game and averaged 9.2 yards per carry and 327.8 yards per game—he broke the national high school rushing record that had stood for 51 years, finishing his four-year career with 12,124 yards, including 4,261 as a senior.

Doing things that others haven't been able to achieve is just a part who he is, and that includes those among the exclusive fraternity of elite running backs at the University of Alabama. The greats who came before Henry—the Humphreys, the Mussos, the Ingrams—they were all in awe of what Henry did.

During his first two seasons at Alabama, Henry remained the *two* in the one-two Crimson Tide running-backs punch. But his junior year he was the undisputed *one*. Henry carried the ball a whopping 395 times in 2015, a mark that ranks first in single-season carries in program history. That's by far the most. Shaun Alexander is second, and he ranks at 93 times fewer in 1999. To say Henry was a workhorse in 2015 is a vast understatement.

Arguably the most remarkable thing in a season full of noteworthy achievements is the oft-overlooked fact that the majority of his success came against his team's most difficult challenges. There was no feasting on the little guys to boost his numbers. So when a game was decided, when Alabama was comfortably ahead, Henry exited the game instead of padding his stats.

Of Henry's school-record 2,219 yards rushing in 2015, 90 percent came against Power 5 opponents. In a total of 12 games against Power 5 competition—composed of Wisconsin, Ole Miss, Georgia, Arkansas, Texas A&M, Tennessee, LSU, Mississippi State, Auburn, Florida, Michigan State, and Clemson—he rushed 355 times for 2,003 yards and 22 of his 28 touchdowns. In other words, he didn't compile his stats against inferior competition; he saved his best for the big boys. That's a trait former Alabama greats think won him the Heisman Trophy. Henry wasn't the front-runner for the entire season; it started when he went for 210 yards and 3 touchdowns against LSU, which had a great running back of its own in Leonard Fournette. Henry stepped up when it mattered most.

"He played his best games against his best competition," former running back Johnny Musso said. "I know how they do it at Alabama—you don't get junk yards when the game is decided or against lesser opponents. When the game is decided, you're out of there. He got his yards the hard way; he got his against the best competition. I really respect that. It all came within the framework of the team's performance and the team's need. He didn't carry the ball 40-something times because they were trying to get him recognition or positioning for the Heisman. They did it because Kenyan Drake was hurt and they needed him every yard and every carry. I really respect the way he earned it." It was in the same year that Henry broke Musso's Iron Bowl record for carries in a game when the junior rushed 46 times for 271 yards.

A lot can be assumed when you're 6'3" and 242 pounds. People assume you should be good just because you're so big. "Henry rushing for 200 yards? Big deal! He should! He's bigger than everyone else." To that end, Henry never rested on his natural ability; he did everything he could to maximize his talent.

During the off-season when he went on spring break before his junior season, Henry went with a few teammates to Panama City, Florida. Henry wanted to break from all the relaxing to put in work. "I just didn't want to miss a beat," Henry said. "We were having fun, but I was like, 'Hey, we gotta get some work in.' So we started doing push-ups, running in the sand, just doing anything to get us a sweat to make us feel good." Then there were the summer workouts during which he flipped tires to improve his strength and endurance.

He arrived with the work ethic when he came to Tuscaloosa. "He always was a hard worker, and he was anxious to improve and try to overcome any deficiencies he had as a player," Nick Saban said.

Everyone recognized the size, but there existed a graceful element to Henry's style of running that one didn't often see in large backs. There were equal parts ballerina and bulldozer. It never really looked like he was running fast; he just sort of glided across the field. He could lower his shoulder and get through a hole, put his thigh pad on your chest, run you over on his way to a long run, using multiple stiff-arms to score. He could also glide around the outside, long-striding, and run past a defensive back.

He was a between-the-tackles runner and a make-you-miss runner, though that largely went unnoticed during his time at Alabama because people saw only his size; it always came back to his size. Bobby Humphrey, Alabama's second-leading career rusher, weighed nearly 60 pounds less than Henry when he played at UA. He marveled at what Henry could do at his size. "He's going to be listed as one of the great ones that played at Alabama, if not possibly the greatest," Humphrey said. "It's simply because there is nobody that has come through with his makeup that is as tall, big, and fast and has all the tangible things like catching the ball out of the backfield, being able to make guys miss in the open field, being able to run with power. He is a one-in-a-lifetime back, a rare back. He [had] all the qualities. There are some backs who are small but who are fast. There are some who are big but not as fast. There are some who can catch. There are some who can't. There are some who can block. There are some who can't. This is a young man who possess[ed] all those skills and really perform[ed] them all very well. I think he is going to be considered one of the greatest backs to ever play at Alabama."

Henry ranks second in career rushing yards in program history. Najee Harris passed him in 2020, though it's only fair to put into context that Harris played four years at Alabama and Henry played three. For his career, Henry averaged six yards every time he carried the football.

His durability was never in question for those around the program. For crying out loud, he carried it 395 times in 2015, including games with carries of 46, 44, 38, and 36 yards. Those outside the program publicly questioned if Alabama was using him up, if the workload was too much for the big man. But it never happened. He only got better the more times he touched the ball. As his opponents got more tired every time they had to tackle him, he just kept going. He maintained while those trying to get him faltered.

He became just the third runner in SEC history to rush for four 200-yard rushing games in the same season. The other two? Herschel Walker and Bo Jackson. Both of those players won the Heisman Trophy too. Henry became the second Alabama player to win the Heisman Trophy. Mark Ingram was the first. They were both running backs. The only running backs to win the award this century are them and Reggie Bush (2005).

Henry has passed every test put in front on him and at every level. Coaches who had to plan to stop him were never shy in their appraisal of Henry. Trying to stop him was a lesson in futility. Onetime Florida coach Jim McElwain—who coached Glen Coffee, Roy Upchurch, Mark Ingram, and Trent Richardson during his four years as Alabama's offensive coordinator—said Henry is in a class by himself. "All I can say is wow," McElwain said. "The speed and the power and really the way Derrick always [went] forward. In a long line of great running backs that were there, I think it's a testament to Coach Saban and what they're committed to doing year in and year out. Getting that guy behind center like that, that can make a difference in any ball game. He [was] definitely a difference maker. We [had] our work cut out for us trying to...slow him down."

Henry was impressive in high school and in college, and continues to be so in the NFL, currently for the Tennessee Titans. At every level he's rushed for at least 2,000 yards in a single season. He's the only player in history to have reached the 2,000-yard mark at each of those levels. He's always been the big man at each step of the way.

8

Barrett Jones

BARRETT JONES IS SO UNASSUMING HE LULLS YOU TO SLEEP
with his kindness. At no point during an interaction with the
affable former Alabama football player would it enter your mind
that this man was one of the most effective offensive linemen in
the program's history. Jones is a nice guy. He's also a formerly
mean guy. Maybe *mean* is not the best way to describe it, but
let's put it this way: If you stood between him and winning, he
wouldn't hesitate to bury you. His competitive fire runs so hot
that he once shoved his own quarterback in the waning minutes
of a clinched national championship game.

He's also a member of a family that one may refer to as
the first family of University of Alabama sports. Barrett won
the Rimington and Outland Trophies and was a two-time All-
American during his five-year Crimson Tide career. His father,
Rex, played basketball for the Crimson Tide. His brothers,
Harrison and Walker, both played football at UA. And for good

measure, his grandfather is a member of the Alabama Sports Hall of Fame.

As a journalist, I was taught early on that objectivity matters, and it does. But it's also impossible to have 100 percent objectivity. We all have biases. The key when being a journalist is to be transparent about those biases with your audience. So here goes: I love the Joneses. They are as nice a family as you'll ever encounter. Despite their seemingly natural athletic ability, they don't let that define them. Barrett won't be rude if you ask him a question about his playing days; it's just that he doesn't need to talk about all that he accomplished. He is completely secure in who he is today, which is a son, brother, husband, and father. He's also not shy about sharing his faith, which has always been a big part of who he is.

To understand how Barrett became one of the most decorated players in Alabama football's rich history, you first need to know his family, especially his parents, Rex and Leslie. They began dating in Rex's sophomore year at Alabama after he'd broken his collarbone. He called Leslie to come visit him, and the romance started in earnest.

"After the first night that we went out, I came home and said I was gonna marry that girl," Rex Jones said. "He asked why. I said, 'Because she cares nothing about sports.'"

There's a certain hilarity in that statement now, considering Rex ended up with a household of college athletes. But that first date led to marriage and three boys. Rex and Leslie provided three things in abundance for Barrett, Harrison, and Walker: respect, faith, and love.

It may be a funny thought now, looking at their size, but Leslie insisted all three boys learn the violin. They played the violin an hour a day. Can you imagine Barrett's big, powerful hands wrapped around a violin? It's comical to think about now.

But early on, sports were not his forte. "He was a Great Dane puppy—big, gangly, tall, and he had trouble keeping his feet up under him," Rex Jones said. "We signed him up for church league basketball in the third grade. Now we're not talking all that competitive; this is just church league. He did not score a point the whole season. Everybody is cheering for him to score, and they'd keep him in the game to let him shoot. And he's the tallest one out there. So I told my wife one night that I really hoped he liked that violin, because he was not gonna play sports."

Each year Barrett got a little better, though. In seventh grade it was like an alarm bell went off. He traveled all over Memphis on teams, and it became evident that the Great Dane had found his footing. That's when Rex started singing a different tune: "I said, 'We got hope.'"

At that point, basketball was Barrett's love, but football crept in. The Joneses' next-door neighbor is Jimmy Sexton. Yes, *that* Jimmy Sexton. One weekend Sexton called Rex and invited him and the family to an LSU–Mississippi State game to watch the game from the sideline. That was the Joneses' first encounter with Nick Saban, then the coach at LSU. It made an impression. "That's the first time my boys ever heard some of that language," Rex joked.

Barrett Jones grew with the game of football. His freshman season at Evangelical Christian, he played defensive end. His sophomore season he started at left tackle. It was a small Christian school, and it was hard to measure how good he actually was. The family really had no way of knowing how to get him noticed. They were a little naive to the recruiting process. That's when Sexton told him to pick three summer football camps and to attend. He chose Auburn, Alabama, and Tennessee. Auburn was first up.

"When we came back to pick him up, he said, 'Coach Tuberville wants to talk to y'all,'" Leslie said. Here's how naive the entire family was to the recruiting process: Rex thought Barrett had done something wrong and gotten in trouble. Barrett, on the other hand, thought the head coach met with every player and family after camp.

Jones had performed well in the offensive-defensive line camp. He'd lost one rep all week, and that came against defensive tackle Ian Williams, who went on to play at Notre Dame. But in his mind, he still had no idea what was about to come.

"So we went up to his office, and one thing I remember that he said was, 'Barrett is a really good football player. He's got all the measurables that he needs to play in college,'" Leslie said. "He offered him a scholarship, and Barrett said, 'You're telling me you're offering me a scholarship to come play football at Auburn?' Then he asked if he could get it in writing. After it was over, we got in the van, and Barrett looked at me and said, 'If I died right now, I'd be happy, because he told me that I'm good enough to play college football.'"

Alabama was up next. Coming on the heels of the Auburn offer, the family sort of expected Alabama to be next. But Alabama didn't offer. Not only did they not offer Barrett; they practically ignored him. "[Head coach Mike] Shula's coming over and talking to me about everything," Rex said. "You know the one thing he didn't talk to me about? He didn't even pay any attention to Barrett. Mark Gottfried was the basketball coach then, and so Mark got to Shula and said, 'You know Auburn's into this kid, right?' And Shula said he didn't know and it didn't really make that much difference to him."

Tennessee was the final camp that summer, and Sexton was there. Coach Phil Fulmer paid Barrett a lot of attention, but

Tennessee didn't offer either, so when the family got back home, Rex said, "Hey, Barrett, looks like we're going to Auburn." That's how the recruitment of Jones began (and for the record, both Alabama and Tennessee eventually offered). But Jones sort of had a bad taste in his mouth with his Alabama experience. And after word of the Auburn offer got out there, other schools were fast to begin their recruitment of him too.

Rex had just sold the family business, and his new job was at Evangelical Christian. The fall of Barrett's junior season in high school was when schools could begin recruiting him off campus. Let's just say that the door to Rex's office stayed busy that fall. Kevin Sumlin, Ed Orgeron, and more wore out a path to his office—all in hopes of Jones signing with their programs. "I met more coaches, head coaches, and assistant coaches, and because I worked at the school, they had complete freedom to feel like they could come and stay as long as they wanted," Rex said.

Under Shula, Alabama did start recruiting Barrett, but the way Alabama did it left a lot to be desired. On a Tennessee game day visit, the family was assigned a hostess who was very professional. At Alabama the hostess basically got them to their seats and then said she had other things to do. The family described it as disorganized. It left such a bad impression that Leslie turned to Rex and said, "I know one place he's *not* going to school."

They'd visited Alabama for the 2006 Mississippi State game, and the players just looked disheveled, were wearing sweat suits that didn't match, and were more concerned with their headphones than anything else. At Tennessee the players wore suits and looked organized. It also didn't help that Alabama lost and the crowd at Bryant-Denny Stadium was flat.

If Nick Saban had not become the Alabama coach the next season, Barrett Jones would have gone to North Carolina to play for Butch Davis. But Saban did come to Alabama and flipped the entire program. *Disorganized* and *Saban* do not belong in the same sentence. He got everything running smoothly, and that ultimately made the difference for Jones.

In 2007 Stanford threw its hat into the ring too. Jim Harbaugh spent many hours recruiting Barrett and even used arguably his biggest win to do so. After Stanford beat Southern California in 2007 as 41-point underdogs, in the locker room during the celebration after the game, Harbaugh called Barrett and left a message: "Barrett, we just beat USC. Jim Harbaugh, Stanford. I just wanted to call and tell you about it. Jim Harbaugh. Come be a part of it. Stanford University."

Barrett saved that message for years. When Jones made his decision to go to Alabama, he called every coach who had recruited him and personally told them. Every coach was friendly and nice, except one: Harbaugh. "He told me I was making a mistake I'd regret for the rest of my life," Barrett said. "I saw him later in my first-ever game I did for ESPN [as a commentator]. It was Michigan-Florida on ESPN Radio. I walk into the coaches meeting, and he looks up at me and says, 'I'm still mad at you.' I said, 'Coach, you left two years later for the 49ers.' And he said, 'Doesn't matter.' I think he's still mad at me."

But Saban and his love of growing up an Alabama fan were too much to pass up. Jones wanted to be a part of it. Little did he know he'd leave the program as a starter at three different positions on the offensive line; with three national championships; as a two-time All-American, Outland Trophy winner, and Rimington Trophy winner; and as a permanent team captain. I mean, how does one dare dream that big? "I would say that honestly...being a captain means the most to me," Barrett Jones said. "And I loved winning the national championships. The team part of it."

That's why the first national championship, the 2009 BCS title, is Jones's favorite of the three he won. You always remember your first. It meant so much to him that after the final second ticked off in the 37–21 victory over Texas, while others were running around the field and hugging each other or heading to the stands to find loved ones, Jones made a beeline for the podium. He'd long dreamed of holding that trophy. He wanted to be one of the first to have a moment with it. "I was strategic," Jones said, laughing.

There were lessons learned after that title too. Alabama lost focus the following season, and a talented team lost three games in 2010—to South Carolina, to LSU, and to Auburn. When the team won it again in 2011, Jones and family basked in the glory of another title at Ruth's Chris Steak House in New Orleans. They celebrated well into the night, and NBA royalty joined them: Charles Barkley sat with the family for a long portion of the night—an Auburn man saluting an Alabama man who'd just won his second national championship.

Not long after that night, though, Nick Saban called his team together and put an end to the past. That began the journey of trying to repeat as champions, a notoriously difficult thing to do in college football. Nebraska had last achieved that in 1994 and '95. Other teams had come close but never finished the job. That's what Alabama wanted to do. When they accomplished it with a complete dismantling of Notre Dame the following season, Jones was the first to call Alabama's run what it truly was: a dynasty. It got picked up from there, but Jones—now out of eligibility—could stop living in the moment for a second and recognize that his team had won two in a row and three out of four. It was a dynasty. And he said it on national television. No college football team since has won two national championships in a row—including

Alabama, which played in four national championships in a row from 2015 to 2018.

"I think honestly we were probably more focused that year on repeating at least our group, because we were all there in 2010," Barrett Jones said. "When [we lost in 2010], we just felt like that was such a letdown of a year. And yeah, like when you're there, you're so brainwashed to focus on just what's right in front of you. I'll never forget, like three days after the national championship [in 2011], before we had even had the parade, Nick Saban called a meeting with the leadership and said, 'No more talk about the championship. We're moving on to 2012.'...So honestly, we were just more focused on that year and repeating. 'Let's repeat; that's hard to do. It's hard to win it twice in a row.' That was all the talk that year."

Then it was over. Jones was drafted and had a brief NFL career. He now works in the private sector around Memphis and does color commentating for college football for ESPN. When Saban sees him in the facility preparing for a game, he tells him to come to his office. When he sees him on the field prior to a game, he sends someone to bring him over. Saban, never the warm and fuzzy type, clearly has a soft spot for Barrett Jones.

Jones was fortunate to grow up in an amazing family who taught him much about faith and love and empathy. Saban's famed Process taught him a lot too—things that he'll one day teach to his son. Jones relies so much on what he learned there that he doesn't know how to turn it off, to the point that it has been problematic. Earlier in their marriage, Barrett's wife, Katie, had to draw the line. "My wife told me early on, 'Hey, I love you so much, but I don't play football for Alabama. So when I'm having a bad day, I don't need you to coach me how to overcome adversity.'"

Jones continued, "But seriously, a lot of what [Saban] taught us sticks with me. Living life not by a comparison but living to a standard. You know, my faith is something that's really important to me, and I think that I've stolen Coach Saban's message many times and applied it as a spiritual message of that, like, 'Hey, your life and your character and who you are [are what matter]. You don't need to just live your life in comparison all the time and say, "Well, I'm better than this guy" or "Look at me. I do a lot better. I give more money away or whatever. I'm morally superior." You live your life to a standard and figure out what you stand for and what you believe in and who you want to be. And so I think there's just unlimited applications to that. I use those things all the time, and everyone jokingly calls me Coach Saban. But I believe all that stuff, I really do. And when I coach my son one day, I'll use it there too."

Jones cast a big shadow for his brothers, whom he calls his favorite teammates. Both played at Alabama. Imagine for a second playing there, and your brother is literally one of the most decorated players ever to do it. That might cause a bit of insecurity. To the point that Harrison almost went to North Carolina and Walker seriously considered Mississippi State. "I never pressured them in any way," Barrett said.

The pull of family legacy was too much, though. Three sons of an Alabama basketball standout played for the greatest college football coach of all time. It's the stuff of dreams, but it's real. It happened for one family.

Athletic ability aside, the Jones family is one of my favorites that I've covered during my time as an Alabama beat writer. I admit that I'm a little biased when it comes to them. I've enjoyed every interaction I've had with Rex, Leslie, Barrett, Harrison, and Walker.

I always admired the way Barrett comported himself in the spotlight. It's not easy to be a star player at Alabama; there are many demands on you. There are advantages, to be sure, but there's also the fact that you're growing up in the spotlight. He did so in a first-class manner—for five years in a program that is unrelenting and can break a person.

Since becoming a father in October 2020, I have often thought about what kind of man I wanted my son to become in this world: A man of faith and love who cared about other people. A man who was fiercely protective of his family. A man like Barrett Jones. I wanted to get to know the Joneses better; a family that had raised three successful young men was something I wanted to study. That's why I chose to write about Barrett. His athletic prowess as a star offensive lineman has been well covered, but the journey to get there has not been. The family remains one of my favorites, and I'm so happy they allowed me to share a part of their story.

9

Derrick Thomas and Will Anderson

WHAT ARE THE ODDS THAT ONE PROGRAM LANDED TWO of the greatest ever to do it at one position? That one college football program could land that type of talent seems unlikely. I'm not talking about Paul W. "Bear" Bryant and Nick Saban, though at this point I don't think any reasonable person could argue they are not the two greatest coaches of all time. But I'm talking about arguably the two greatest pass rushers in college football history: Derrick Thomas and Will Anderson.

Going into the 2021 season, there was substantial discussion about whether Anderson, just a sophomore at the time, was the next Thomas. At the time, it seemed nearly sacrilegious to compare the two. Not that Anderson wasn't obviously talented. Even Alabama haters couldn't deny his gifts. It's just that Thomas was in a league all his own. How could he not be? He recorded 27 sacks in 1988. That's not a typo: 27 sacks. In one season. Absurd.

That's why any player, no matter how incredibly talented, being compared to Thomas seemed out of touch. We live in an era biased toward the person to do something most recently; there exists a lack of appreciation for things and events of the past. So comparing Anderson, who was coming off an outstanding freshman season, to Thomas, who literally wrote the book on pressuring the quarterback at the college level, seemed off. But maybe it's not.

I recognized Anderson's talent early on. I'd heard reports coming out of the program about him before his freshman season. That's not exactly novel. Alabama recruits at such a high level that many freshmen are heralded before they have taken a snap of real, actual Alabama football. Anderson backed it up, though. His freshman year he earned the Shaun Alexander Freshman of the Year Award, given out by the Football Writers Association of America. He had 10.5 tackles for loss and 7 sacks. Not bad for a senior, never mind a freshman, but not exactly Derrick Thomas level. Then came Anderson's 2021 sophomore season.

It's hard to put into context just how dominant he was in 2021. He was the best player on Alabama's defense and certainly it's most dominant. While his offensive teammate Bryce Young won the Heisman Trophy, the fact that Anderson didn't make it to New York was nearly criminal. Football analysts from around the country were outraged, and rightfully so. Anderson was flat-out dominant. He compiled 102 tackles with an incredible 34.5 tackles for loss and 17.5 sacks. Really think about that stat line for a second. More than a third of his tackles were tackles for loss. That's insane. And the 17.5 sacks? It's the third most in a single season for an Alabama player.

The top two? You guessed it: They came from Derrick Thomas, with 27 in 1988 and 18 in 1987. That's pretty rarefied air, and why it's not so crazy to compare Anderson to Thomas. You get the feeling that Thomas would love to watch Anderson play. Thomas, who died in 2000, would likely be his biggest fan.

Though he's played only two seasons, Anderson ranks fourth on the program's all-time sacks list (through the 2021 season). He currently trails Kindal Moorehead by half a sack for third and Jonathan Allen by 4.0 and Thomas by an incredible 27.5. NFL scouts told me that had Anderson been draft eligible following his sophomore season, he would have been the No. 1 pick in the draft. In other words, it is incredibly unlikely that Anderson will stick around another two years to have a real shot at breaking Thomas's 52-sack program record.

It's clear for all to see that his talent is immense, but it's the mental makeup that makes him such a special talent. "I think what sets anybody apart is 'What's your mindset?'" Saban said. "How important is it to you? How are you willing to edit your behavior to accomplish the goals that you have? You're going to get out of it what you put into it. Will's A+ in all those intangible areas, plus he's got really good physical ability. The guy is an overachiever even at that...because of the mindset that he has. He's a great effort player, he's very conscientious, he does his job well in the game, he doesn't make a lot of mistakes, he prepares well for every game. So I think it's always the intangible things that help you get to your full potential. Will's certainly got great intangibles with great ability, and that certainly makes for great players."

Anderson (from Hampton, Georgia) and Thomas (from Miami, Florida) grew up differently. Anderson comes from a large family, comprising his parents, Tereon and Will Sr., five older sisters, and an older brother. His grandmother was also instrumental in his life growing up. Thomas grew up without his father, who was a pilot shot down over Vietnam in 1972. That event shaped so much about Thomas's life. He spent much of his adult life obsessed with airplanes and trying to learn more about his father.

Thomas was a naturally gifted pass rusher, and that was clear to everyone who watched him at Alabama. To his coaches and his teammates, he was nearly a superhero sent to earth to attack opposing quarterbacks. "It's not a misprint," former UA coach Bill Curry said. "It's real. His numbers were superhuman. He had leverage, speed, and power to give him an almost unfair advantage over any ordinary mortal that tried to block him."

The Chiefs selected Thomas fourth overall in 1989, and he helped them to nine straight winning seasons. "He was a nightmare for people who had to prepare for him, because he had unique skill," former Kansas City head coach Marty Schottenheimer said.

Thomas passed away when he was 33, his life and career cut short when he died as a result of trauma and complications from a car accident. That makes what he did in such a relatively short period of time so remarkable. Even so, his numbers in the NFL put him in the Hall of Fame. His 126.5 career sacks and 41 forced fumbles are evidence of one of the best pass rushers the game has ever seen. And his 52 sacks with the Crimson Tide helped him into the College Football Hall of Fame. It was that special 1988 season at Alabama that caused a stir, and everyone took notice, including the Kansas City Chiefs.

For Anderson, it's been a career of success from an early age. His junior season—in a different era of college football than Thomas's 1988 junior season—stands on its own too.

It can be argued that rushing the passer and getting him on the ground is as difficult as it's ever been. Quarterbacks are groomed in passing offenses as soon as they reach high school. They enter college much more polished than were those of previous generations. Then there's the spread, wide receiver screens, jet sweeps, and RPOs that help to get the ball out of the quarterback's hand as fast as ever. To get to the quarterback in this era, you have to have an unbelievably quick step. Anderson has that. Without it, it's the difference between a quarterback hurry and a quarterback sack.

In many ways, he was built for this moment. He used internal motivation to set him apart. He had the talent, of course, but he also put in the work. He's added a mental strength to those attributes during his time in the Alabama program, and it has all combined to make him the best defensive player in the country.

Early in his freshman season, Anderson was frustrated. He'd been the talk of the off-season, the sort of can't-miss prospect who cycles through Alabama every couple of years. Glowing reports spilled out of preseason camp, causing those who hadn't yet seen him to salivate about watching him terrorize quarterbacks. But success didn't immediately materialize the way he thought it would. Anderson went into a shell. He was paralyzed by his thoughts, fearful of making a mistake and taking the brunt of a Nick Saban rear-end chewing.

In his first five games, Anderson didn't show many flashes of what made him such a sought-after recruit and a day-one starter. He had just one tackle for loss and no sacks. Stats aren't the only metric to determine production, though, and Anderson had plenty of pressures. It just wasn't what he expected. But he'd earned the Crimson Tide's starting Jack linebacker job for a reason and needed to be reminded of who he was.

So he called his former coach at Dutchtown High School, Clifford Fedd, and he called his father, Will Anderson Sr. As usual, they set him straight. They told him the same thing: Relax. "He wasn't making plays, right?" Fedd said. "He was extremely frustrated. He was beating himself up pretty hard."

Around midseason, Anderson's confidence grew. He relaxed and became more comfortable. A switch flipped. He went from zero sacks in his first seven games to finishing third in the SEC with seven for the season. He was named the Football Writers Association of America Freshman of the Year and earned conference and national championship rings.

He then had an unreal sophomore season—a season so dominant that it led to SEC Defensive Player of the Year honors and the Bronko Nagurski Trophy. He finished fifth in the Heisman Trophy voting too, earning 31 first-place votes. So imagine what the expectations will be going forward, climbing higher and higher. But the highest expectations for Anderson are internal. "I'm always harder on myself," Anderson said. "I'm probably my worst critic. I'm probably harder on myself than my coaches, anybody, because of the expectations I have for myself and the standard I have to hold myself to. That's just how I am in my mentality."

When Anderson was growing up, his parents emphasized hard work and education above all else. They supported and nurtured his athletic dreams. At the same time, his competitive character was stoked by his five older sisters: Shawnta, Shanice, Chyna, Endia, and Teria. They kept him on his toes physically but more so mentally. In many ways, the Anderson sisters motivated their baby brother to always push himself to do more. "They most definitely did," Anderson said. "They made some days hell. I will not lie to you. Some games they came to, all I heard was, 'What are you doing? You're supposed to be doing this? You're not running fast enough. You look like crap.' So I can most definitely say they shaped me into the athlete I am today. I appreciate them a lot. My sisters really pushed me a lot, just watching them how they grind, how they work hard, their work ethic. I just always wanted to be better than them because I think that's what they wanted for me."

Anderson hated football at first, because he wasn't very good at it. He spent practices being the pincushion. He played defensive tackle and on the offensive line, and he had no success other than being on the receiving end of hits. "I used to suck at football when I was little—literally, I was terrible," Anderson said. "I was horrible."

He spent more time pulling grass out of the field and getting yelled at by coaches than he did actually trying to get better. The turning point came in middle school, after a collision with Kevon Glenn, now a linebacker at Georgia Southern. "One practice, he was bullying me," Anderson said. "He had just made snot come out my nose. It was bad. I was crying, like I really didn't want to play football no more. I think after he did that, I was like, 'OK, you know what? *I'm* gonna be the hammer. I'm tired of being the nail.' After that, they moved me to linebacker, and I just started hitting people for no reason. Even if you didn't have the ball, I started hitting you. That's when I think football kind of became fun for me."

That led to a little disagreement within the house. "Big Will used to tell Will, 'You know, on the field is where you get to hit people for free,'" said Tereon Anderson, Will's mother. "I used to think that was such a terrible thing to say. But I think it just kind of stuck with him."

All five of Will's sisters played sports: One played only softball. Another played only volleyball. One ran track and played volleyball. And the other two played volleyball and basketball. When they were younger, they'd have Will set the ball at the net in volleyball so they could practice spiking. Or they'd have him play defense so they could perfect driving to the rim in basketball. "They were rough on him," Will Sr. said. "The first thing I told these girls was, 'All right, y'all might get him crying picking on him now, but one day he's going to be bigger than all of y'all.'"

Basketball was Anderson's second sport until an injury led to his concentrating on football. That's when he dedicated himself fully to getting better. No one could have known then what his future held, but the only goal was to outwork everyone else. His parents hired two trainers to work on his outside pass rush, including footwork and hand placement, and he had dedicated training to get faster. On every spring break and winter holiday break, he'd message his high school coach to make sure he'd get extra work in. "It really became a passion for him, and he put his all into it," Fedd said.

The hard work started paying off during his junior season in high school. Against Jones County High School, he had five sacks and a quarterback pressure that forced an interception. He had the game-clinching sack facing a double-team with the running back chipping him, dragging the quarterback down with one arm. "That was unbelievable," Dutchtown High School defensive coordinator Will Rogers said. "At that point, he said, 'We're not going to lose.' He'd made his mind up that we weren't going to lose.... I cried at his graduation. I really wish we had him this year."

As Anderson's final season in high school approached, Fedd took his seniors to Stone Mountain for a team-building outing. On the way back down the mountain, those seniors ran into an area of people working out and competing in a tug-of-war. A couple of the stronger-looking guys came over to the team and challenged them. Fedd picked out the biggest of the guys and said, "I've got someone for you." He told Anderson to get ready. "Will Anderson went from a guy with a smile on his face to a big frown like you were flipping a switch," Fedd said. "He went from a guy having a good time with his team to a guy who was ready for competition. He didn't say a word. He got into a tug-of-war match with a grown man. I'm talking about a full-grown man. This guy was yoked up like he lived in the weight room. And Will drug that man; he drug him with that rope. He has a competition switch that he cuts on and cuts off."

Those who know Anderson best stress that the player on the field is different from the person away from it. He's a family man, fiercely protective of his parents, sisters, grandmother, and older brother, Shawn. His grandmother helped instill his love of fishing. If you want to experience the real Anderson as a competitor, tell him about the biggest fish you've caught and watch him show you a picture that puts the size of your fish to shame.

As a kid, he volunteered for Meals on Wheels with his family. He still loves participating in Habitat for Humanity. It's important to him to treat others the way he wants to be treated. That core belief was taught to him at home as a child. "We didn't have to do a lot of convincing with Will that giving back was important," Tereon Anderson said. "He wanted to do those things. We always stressed, 'To whom much is given, much is required.'"

For Will, it's all about not embarrassing the family. It's always been that way. He never wanted to do anything to bring a bad name to his mom, dad, and grandmother. "I just think it goes back to my parents and my grandmother, and how they raised me—you know, what's right is right, what's wrong is wrong," Anderson said. "What you do to other people will come back to you. And they always told us to treat people with respect. ... We were raised with, 'Yes, ma'am. No, sir.'"

It extends to every area of his life. Anderson doesn't consider himself a superstar, and he concentrates on the process rather than the result. When he made the dean's list for the fall semester of his freshman year at Alabama, he didn't tell anyone. He didn't post it on social media. When his high school coach found out about it, he messaged Anderson to congratulate him. "I said, 'Why didn't you tell me?'" Fedd said. "He said, 'You don't brag about something you're supposed to do.' That's Will, man."

Dutchtown High School's colors are red and black, and its nickname is the Bulldogs. It's only fitting that Anderson, a five-star recruit rated as one of the top players in the country, would have had interest in the home-state Georgia Bulldogs. But during the majority of his recruitment, Kirby Smart's staff never gave him the green light to commit. The staff prioritized other players. It allowed linebackers coach Sal Sunseri and Alabama, with Nick Saban as the closer, to pluck Anderson out of the Peach State.

"To be honest, he went up to Georgia a couple of times to camp," Fedd said. "For whatever reason, they didn't pull the trigger on him, you know? He didn't fit what they wanted. From my understanding, the outside 'backer spot, they wanted somebody that was a little more flexible, able to cover in space, and then the D-end spot; I think he was a little undersized for what they wanted. So therefore they didn't understand or figure out how they wanted to use him.

"No knock to them and their program and what they do, but Alabama knew that they wanted to use him as a pass-rush specialist. Get him out and cover every now and then, but his bang for the buck is going to be getting to that quarterback."

Alabama's scouting turned out to be on the money. After the drought in the first half of his freshman season, Anderson broke out down the stretch, saying he "had to relax and just take a few steps back and just play football." He racked up seven sacks in a four-game run against Auburn, LSU, Arkansas, and Florida to close the regular season. Of 333 total pass-rush opportunities his freshman year, he recorded a pressure about 20 percent of the time, according to Sports Info Solutions. His 60 total pressures in those 13 games are more than any UA player over the past five seasons, including Quinnen Williams's 57 pressures in 15 games in 2018.

Everything lies in front of him, even as more attention bounds his way. He's been a national defensive award winner, an SEC Defensive Player of the Year award winner, and an All-American. What's next? Nothing seems out of reach for him. But just as consistently as the praise rolls in, Anderson remains true to his humble beginnings and shrugs it off. He's just not comfortable discussing himself as a star despite the high expectations being heaped upon him—including from his head coach, a notoriously tough person to please.

"Will is probably the guy that creates more havoc for the defense in terms of his ability to pass rush," Nick Saban said. "He's a more complete player now and understands the whole scheme. He's very diverse as a player in terms of what he can do.

"He's the kind of person that he's not satisfied with where he is. He works hard every day, and he's always trying to get better. I love working with this guy. I think he sets a great example for everybody else on our team."

As the praise comes in from fans, media, and even Saban, there's little concern that it will go to his head. No one is harder on Anderson than himself. He knows his sisters will always be there to motivate him too. Take last season's Kentucky game. Anderson recorded only one tackle and was excited to see his sisters afterward. They let him have it. "You know, once the game was over, there's our second daughter, Shanice, and the first thing she said was, 'Woo, baby, you came out a little slow,'" Tereon Anderson said. "And then Chyna, number three, she was like, 'Yeah, baby, we didn't know what was going on with you. We thought you were missing your parents.'

"But it was just funny because after every game, that's kind of the assessment. It's never: 'Will, did you have a good game?' Or: 'Hey, good job.' It's: 'You missed a tackle.' It's always been some type of assessment as to whether he did good or bad."

Anderson doesn't shy away from what's expected of him because, quite frankly, he expects more of himself. It's just that he doesn't overly concern himself with what outside expectations may be. He's still the kid trying to earn the respect of his biggest fans: his family. "They set good examples, and they expect the same from me," Anderson said. "I think it was all just from their character, how they were raised and how I see them working in their lives every day. Like my dad—his job and how much hard work he has to do. So that was instilled in us. And we put that into sports."

It's not so wild to compare Anderson to Thomas now. That in and of itself is remarkable. For years people speculated about who would be the next Thomas. It eventually was just accepted that there wouldn't *be* another Thomas. It wasn't that there weren't talented individuals who had the game to warrant comparisons to Thomas; it was just that the game had changed and, let's face it, Thomas was a unicorn. He was a pass-rushing unicorn. He was special. So comparing anyone to him felt almost unfair to the player. But people have made those comparisons with Anderson, and they don't feel forced. He's just as talented in his own right. However, Will Anderson is Will Anderson and Derrick Thomas is Derrick Thomas. Both are spectacularly talented. Now, who's going to be the next Will Anderson?

10

The Quarterbacks

THE LAST THREE STARTING QUARTERBACKS AT ALABAMA started for NFL franchises in 2021, and two of three—Mac Jones and Jalen Hurts—started playoff games. The other, Tua Tagovailoa, helped his team, the Miami Dolphins, to a 9–8 record in 2021. It's been quite a run for Crimson Tide signal callers over the past five years. Throw in Bryce Young, the first quarterback from the program to win the Heisman Trophy, and we're in the midst of a Crimson Tide quarterback renaissance.

It didn't start in the Saban era, of course—there's Bart Starr and Joe Namath and Kenny Stabler. But whether because of the talent level of the players brought in or the lack of their development, there was a dry period in top-tier Alabama quarterbacks spanning from Jeff Rutledge in 1987 to AJ McCarron in 2015. For a program that values college football like it does, that span is a long time in the desert. There's absolutely nothing wrong with being a game manager, and many Crimson Tide quarterbacks have been saddled with that label as if it were a negative. Those quarterbacks leaned on the running game, relied on the play-action pass, and were tasked with not turning the ball over.

The level of play at quarterback has been sufficiently raised in the last half decade. It's coincided with the Crimson Tide's change in offensive identity. Since embracing the spread, RPOs, etc., the talent for the skill-position players has grown exponentially. Wide receivers want to play with great quarterbacks, and quarterbacks want to go to a school where there are multiple great targets to throw the ball to. But which came first? Was it the chicken or the egg?

Especially during the Saban era, the elite wide receivers came before the elite quarterbacks. Saban signed Julio Jones, who is a pretty good bet to be a future NFL Hall of Fame member, in his first full recruiting class in 2008. Jones played with John Parker Wilson and Greg McElroy, both of whom made NFL rosters but were never full-time starters. Then came Amari Cooper, a no-doubt superstar wide receiver. He played with AJ McCarron and Blake Sims. McCarron is still in the NFL but has never been a franchise's full-time starter.

What came next set the stage for historic offenses that went from averaging 35 points per game in 2015 to averaging more than 45 points per game over the last four seasons. What happened was Jerry Jeudy, Henry Ruggs III, DeVonta Smith, Jaylen Waddle, John Metchie, and Jameson Williams were catching passes from Tua Tagovailoa, Mac Jones, and Bryce Young.

It's led to historic quarterback play at Alabama. All three of those quarterbacks have been Heisman Trophy finalists, and one was a winner. The Alabama quarterback ratings since 2018 are as follows: 199.4, 206.9, 203.1, and 167.5.

Jalen Hurts did some nice things as the starting quarterback in 2016 and 2017, but Tagovailoa really started the elite passing game. His skills transcended what was seen before and easily showed the Crimson Tide's passing game had gone to the next level. "He does a nice job of keeping his eyes downfield, stepping up in the pocket," Saban said. "There were a couple of third-down plays where he bought some time, stepped up in the pocket, and we were able to convert on throws. He's well prepared, but he's also very instinctive and he does a good job of keeping his eyes downfield to find people in the middle."

Tagovailoa made it look so easy. He was the story of the college football season in 2018, and it's still sort of unreal that his injury in the 2018 SEC Championship Game cost him a Heisman Trophy. Before that game, it was his award to win. He threw 43 touchdowns against 6 interceptions that season, but the throw of the season came at Tennessee when Tagovailoa hit Jaylen Waddle on a crossing route for a 77-yard touchdown pass, floating the ball over the two Volunteers defenders. Mouths fell open in the press box; we all knew we were watching greatness.

"It's just incredible. It's so good it makes you sick sometimes," former Mississippi State quarterback Matt Wyatt told me. "You try your best as an analyst not to overstate anything because you don't want to blow something out of proportion, so I'm careful, but I'm just not sure that I've seen a quarterback as a sophomore with overall limited snaps as a freshman that processes everything the way he does, as quickly as he processes it. The anticipation of a defense, the ball coming out on time every time it seems like, and no hesitation whatsoever in throwing receivers. I was seeing that on tape last year. He's doing it even more this year.... He does some things that you can't coach. He's [uncannily] accurate. He's really just incredible."

Mac Jones wasn't as physically talented as Tagovailoa, but he was smart and accurate, two skills that made his 2020 season one for the record books. His 41–4 touchdowns-to-interceptions ratio was off the charts in a season in which he only played against Power 5 defenses. In any other year, he would've been the recipient of the Heisman Trophy. Instead, it went to his teammate and top receiver DeVonta Smith.

Jones moved well within the pocket to avoid the rush, and again, he was extremely accurate. That accuracy let him throw the ball down the field for big plays, hitting receivers in stride to maximize yards after the catch. He went from being doubted in the off-season, with some questioning whether freshman Bryce Young could earn the job, to being a first-round draft pick. Not bad for a guy who waited on the bench for three years before his turn came.

Jones came on to end the 2019 Crimson Tide season after Tagovailoa suffered a season-ending hip injury against Mississippi State. In tough circumstances, Jones showed some signs of what was to come in 2020, but no one expected what he did.

Even as Jones was in the midst of that truly historical 2020 season, college and pro football analysts alike attributed much of his success to Smith and Waddle. It was almost as if people were looking to discredit what he was doing, which created great uncertainty regarding where exactly Jones would be drafted. In the days leading up to the draft, there was legitimate talk that he would be drafted early by the San Francisco 49ers. That talk led to many articles almost incredulous that Jones could go that high, and the rhetoric grew all the more angry when it was suggested he might go before dual-threat quarterback Justin Fields of Ohio State.

Saban had only great things to say about Jones leading up to the draft. "Well, I think if you just watch Mac play throughout the course of the year, if it came to mental errors, he only made a few," Saban said. "He was always very well prepared. I think [Steve Sarkisian] did a great job with them.... [Jones] went out there and calmly just executed and took what the defense gave him and made the right choices and decisions based on what we had coached him to do. Seldom did he force the ball. Seldom did he turn it over. [He] really managed exactly what we expected him to manage, and I know that when you say a guy does that, everybody thinks he's not a very good player, he's not capable of anything else but managing. But to me, to be a good quarterback, you [have] to be a good manager, then your ability to make plays goes from there. And Mac has the ability to make plays because he's smart, he's accurate, he's gonna throw the ball in the right place, and he's gonna always help the offensive team...whether it's a run or a pass or whatever."

It worked out for Jones, of course. It's only fitting that he was drafted by the New England Patriots, coached by Saban's mentor and former boss Bill Belichick. Jones locked down the starting job before the season opener, with the team releasing former NFL MVP Cam Newton.

After two consecutive Alabama starting quarterbacks were drafted in the first round, the next player up was Bryce Young, who earned the starting job at quarterback in 2021. How could a first-year starter fill the shoes of his two predecessors, especially without having the caliber of wide receivers and offensive line the previous two did? John Metchie and Jameson Williams had excellent seasons, but Alabama didn't roll out targets in the same numbers as when Tagovailoa and Jones had been QB. Even tight end Jahleel Billingsley, who was projected to have a big season in 2021, wasn't reliable. Young made the most of Metchie and Williams, working behind an inconsistent offensive line to win the Heisman Trophy.

He did so with a performance that will stand the test of time. Alabama won the SEC championship against a historically good Georgia defense that was viewed an impenetrable before Young carved them up. That game unquestionably proved Young was the best player in college football as Alabama handed Georgia its first and only loss of the season. His line from the game: 26 of 44 passing for 421 yards and three touchdowns and a rushing touchdown. But he had been exceptional at keeping Alabama relevant all season long. Without him, it's possible the Crimson Tide would have lost four or more games.

Saban knows what he has in Young. "Bryce does about as good a job as anybody we've ever had in our program in terms of how he prepares for a game, how he studies the other team, how he sort of knows the ins and outs of what we want to try to execute and what we want to try to do on offense," Saban said. "He's well-liked by his teammates. He's a leader, and he's got sort of an emotional stability about him that he doesn't really get frustrated or upset in any kind of way even when things don't go well. He can stay focused and keep doing what he thinks he needs to do to be able to have success and make adjustments, adapt to what he needs to do. He's a very, very mature guy, way beyond his years in terms of how he views what he needs to do to be successful. And he's pretty committed to it and has a single-minded purpose in trying to get it done. And I think it does impact and affect other players on the offensive side of the ball."

Him being well-liked by his teammates is especially noteworthy. Young was voted as the most valuable player for 2021 and, more importantly for those within the program, was made a permanent team captain. That was voted on by his teammates, and it speaks volumes about what the team thinks of him. It's not often that a sophomore gets that honor, but it tells a certain story about Young and his role on this particular team. It was a young, inexperienced team, and although quarterbacks are stereotypically expected to lead, that can be awkward for a younger player, especially when you have veterans such as left tackle Evan Neal and wide receiver John Metchie in the same huddle. But Young welcomed it. He knew the team needed it.

Quarterbacks at Alabama were once labeled as game managers, and even though that sort of describes what's expected from a quarterback, it was used as a negative descriptor for Crimson Tide signal callers. But no more. Now Alabama quarterbacks manage games and win them with their passing.

PART 3

BUILDING THE TEAMS

11

Ranking the Saban teams

Talk about your thankless tasks. Nick Saban currently captains the most successful dynasty in the history of college football, a dynasty that gets more expansive by the year. So it's no easy task to rank the teams under his stewardship, from his first in 2007 to his most recent in 2021. It's an intriguing exercise, though, because you must account for shifts in the game, and each team must be viewed through the prism of that particular year in the sport. I've been around for each of Saban's 15 seasons, and what follows is my ranking of those teams, from best to worst.

No. 1: 2020
This team holding down the top spot might be the most anticlimactic No. 1 of all time. It's arguably the greatest college

football team of all time, and its list of accomplishments reads as such.

It's the only team in Southeastern Conference history to win 11 conference games. The out-of-conference schedule got dumped due to COVID-19, and instead they faced a daunting conference opponent week after week after week. And they rolled right through it. The only time this team seemed mortal was in the SEC Championship Game against a talented Florida offense that pushed the Crimson Tide until the final second ticked off the clock inside Mercedes-Benz Stadium.

Even with that schedule of only Power 5 opponents, the team averaged 48.5 points per game and scored 84 touchdowns, 15 more than the next-closest team. Three players from this offense finished in the top five of Heisman Trophy voting with wide receiver DeVonta Smith winning the award, quarterback Mac Jones finishing third, and running back Najee Harris finishing fifth.

Off the field, the team dealt with as much distraction as possible with COVID swirling all around it. Daily testing, contract testing, the constant churn of worrying about games being canceled or postponed, and no spring practice all combined to create a environment like few others in the history of the sport.

Coaches missed games after testing positive. Saban tested positive twice, once against Georgia in what turned about to be a false positive. The other against Auburn, which he did miss. Offensive coordinator Steve Sarkisian took the head coaching responsibilities for that game. The LSU game was postponed because of COVID numbers and made up as the second-to-last regular-season game.

This team was able to get through so many distractions because of two factors: talent and leadership. It tied the NFL

Draft record of having six players go in the first round of the 2021 draft, with Jaylen Waddle, DeVonta Smith, Mac Jones, Najee Harris, Alex Leatherwood, and Patrick Surtain II all selected. Five of those were offensive players, which helps explain the offensive success in 2020. In terms of leadership, the seniors led the way with Smith, Landon Dickerson, Leatherwood, Harris, and Dylan Moses.

Saban has had lots of success in his decade and a half in Tuscaloosa, but this team stands out, which says something. Even Saban, who does not often wax poetic about the greatness of his teams, couldn't hold back regarding the excellence this team had. "Well, to me, this team accomplished more almost than any team," Saban said. "No disrespect to any other teams that we had or any championship teams. But this team won 11 SEC games. No other team has done that. They won the SEC, went undefeated in the SEC, then they beat two great teams in the playoffs with no break in between. Played 13 games and went undefeated with all the disruption that we had in this season. I think there's quite a bit to write about when it comes to the legacy of the team."

No. 2: 2009

In his third year as the Crimson Tide head coach, Saban struck gold, going unbeaten in the BCS era and hauling in the first of six national championships at Alabama.

That 14–0 team was led by defense and a power running game. It was the sign of what was to come for Saban and Alabama, a formula only a change of the game could alter. The hurry-up, no-huddle offense and changing of the rules to allow offensive linemen to be up to three yards down the field ushered in the run-pass option (RPO); before then Alabama ruled college football the way a python rules its habitat: pure suffocation.

The Crimson Tide ran the ball and stopped the run. It wasn't viewed as an especially exciting style of football to watch for non-Alabama fans, but it was effective. With a No. 2–ranked total defense, Alabama eked out enough offense to run the table for a perfect season. It's one of only two perfect seasons for Saban at Alabama.

There's no doubt that there are other Alabama teams in the Saban era that were better than this group, but for its time, it was special enough to go unbeaten. It's also the first Alabama team to do so. There's something to be said for being the first. And even with the championships that followed, it remained the only unbeaten team at Alabama until 2020.

The season also produced the program's first Heisman Trophy winner when running back Mark Ingram rode the status of being the best offensive player on the best team to make history for UA. "It's real special for our entire team and our entire organization," Ingram said. "Since we lost to Utah last year, Coach said, 'What do you want to be remembered as?' Well, we had our mind set on going undefeated and winning the national championship and winning the SEC championship. Just the fact that we went out there and we worked every day and we had a common goal that we wanted to accomplish, it's real sweet that we're here and we took advantage of the opportunity. We're obviously proud and excited and can't wait to get back to Tuscaloosa and celebrate with the rest of Alabama and the rest of our team."

It was the first national championship in 17 years, since Gene Stallings's 1992 group that also led with defense. In that way, the teams sort of paralleled the other in the style of play.

After this season, Saban's statue took its place outside the north side of Bryant-Denny Stadium with other national championship–winning coaches. Since then he's added 2011, 2012, 2015, 2017, and 2020 to the inscriptions alongside 2009.

Even more so than the win over Texas in the national title game, this season is best remembered for Alabama's victory over No. 1 Florida in the SEC title game. The Gators ended Alabama's unbeaten season the year before, and the Crimson Tide returned the favor by soundly beating Tim Tebow and the mighty Gators 32–13.

No. 3: 2012

One thing you must confront when undertaking these rankings is how you treat the championship seasons. In other words, you must have the internal debate about whether or not teams that won championships are actually better than teams that did not. There's no perfect formula for this, at least not for me, but I tended to weigh championship teams with higher regard than those that came close but didn't win. This thought process will come into focus later in the list, but for now, there's no debating how good the 2012 team was.

It was a team that lost only once, to Johnny Manziel and Texas A&M, and even in that game, Alabama had the ball late in the fourth quarter with a chance to win. Aside from that, there were a lot of blowouts and three memorable games.

The first was the comeback at LSU when quarterback AJ McCarron hit running back T. J. Yeldon on a screen pass for a game-winning 28-yard touchdown with less than a minute remaining. That play has been played over and over on the big screens inside Bryant-Denny Stadium and cemented its place in Crimson Tide history. The win preserved the team's No. 1 ranking, but the loss to the Aggies a week later cast uncertainty over the season. The team finished the regular season with a pair of 49–0 wins before facing Georgia in the SEC Championship Game.

It was arguably the best SEC Championship Game ever, and it came down to the final play. Alabama had taken the lead in the fourth quarter with a deep touchdown pass to freshman wide receiver Amari Cooper down the left sideline. But Georgia had some late theatrics of their own, driving down to the Alabama 5 with only seconds remaining. Instead of clocking the ball to preserve time on the clock, Georgia quarterback Aaron Murray threw a back-shoulder pass to the end zone. But UA linebacker C. J. Mosley tipped the ball and it fell into a Bulldogs receiver's hands and the clock hit zero to earn a thrilling win.

Then in the BCS National Championship Game, Alabama trounced unbeaten Notre Dame to earn Saban's third national championship. Running back Eddie Lacy rushed for 140 yards and a touchdown, Yeldon ran for 108 yards and a touchdown, and McCarron threw for four touchdowns in the 42–14 win.

The win gave Alabama its third national championship in a four-year period, leading to talk of a dynasty. Not even Saban would dampen that talk, which speaks to what the program had accomplished. "I think it's pretty special what we've accomplished—what the players accomplished, what the coaches accomplished—I think it's really special," Saban said. "And one of these days when I'm sitting on the side of a hill watching the stream go by, I'll probably figure it out even more. But what about next year's team? You've got to think about that too."

The next year's team was on the brink of history, until… we'll get to that soon.

No. 4: 2016

This is the team that was the most fun for me to cover. It didn't win a national championship, but it's more talented and a better team than some that did. That's why it's ranked higher than three teams that won a national championship, which I'm sure won't be controversial at all.

Let's start with the characters and talent on the defense. Just take a look at the draft picks from this defense:

Jonathan Allen, defensive lineman, drafted in the first round

Daron Payne, defensive lineman, drafted in the first round

Dalvin Tomlinson, defensive lineman, drafted in the second round

Tim Williams, linebacker, drafted in the third round

Reuben Foster, linebacker, drafted in the first round

Shaun Dion Hamilton, linebacker, drafted in the sixth round

Rashaan Evans (who played when Hamilton got injured), linebacker, drafted in the first round

Ryan Anderson, linebacker, drafted in the second round

Marlon Humphrey, cornerback, drafted in the first round

Anthony Averett, cornerback, drafted in the fourth round

Minkah Fitzpatrick, cornerback, drafted in the first round

Eddie Jackson, safety, drafted in the fourth round

Ronnie Harrison, safety, drafted in the third round

Look at the caliber of players at every level of the defense. There are six first-rounders on the list. Matching the personality of their defensive coordinator Jeremy Pruitt, the group was aggressive. They brought pressure up the middle with Jonathan Allen and Dalvin Tomlinson and off the edge by Tim Williams and Ryan Anderson. They helped sack the quarterback 54 times.

If that's not enough to sufficiently impress the hardest of hearts, consider these stats. It was the No. 1 scoring defense, the No. 1 rushing defense, and No. 1 in total defense. The defense returned 6 interceptions and 5 fumbles for a total of 11 touchdowns. That alone is worthy of marvel.

Clearly the defense could hold its own with any of the Alabama greats. But the offense led the SEC in scoring with a freshman quarterback at the helm in Jalen Hurts. Hurts didn't make the first start in the season opener against Southern California (Blake Barnett started that game), but he did take over in the first quarter and never gave the job back.

With Lane Kiffin as the offensive coordinator, Hurts thrived in the offense. He led a memorable comeback in Oxford, Mississippi, with the team down 24–3 just before the half. Alabama had another close game in Baton Rouge against LSU, with Hurts scoring the game's only touchdown in a 10–0 Crimson Tide win. And Hurts gave Alabama a lead over Clemson in the national championship game late in the fourth quarter.

But the defense, which played 99 total plays, couldn't hold up as Deshaun Watson led Clemson down the field and scored a touchdown with a second remaining to break hearts on the Alabama sideline. To this day, it's the most distraught locker room I've ever covered. When I asked Ryan Anderson for an interview after the game, he looked at me, smiled, and said, "You don't want to interview a grown man who's crying."

I choose to remember that team for what it was: greatness. What that team accomplished stands to this day even without a title. What if Eddie Jackson and Bo Scarbrough hadn't gotten injured? What if Lane Kiffin hadn't been relieved of his duties before the national championship game? A lot of what-ifs, but that's hindsight. The team remains one of Alabama's best.

"I will remember this team as a group of winners, great competitors, guys that showed tremendous resiliency throughout this season," Saban said. "In some of the games we got down in, some of the games we didn't play very well, they kept coming back. It was demonstrated in this game today. We got behind 28–24 and the offense went down and found a way to score to get us ahead 31–28 to give us a chance to win. We just didn't get them stopped defensively. So I think the perseverance and the resiliency that this team has showed certainly makes them winners in my book, and I'll always remember them for that."

No. 5: 2011

Speaking of defense, the 2011 team stands alone in modern college football. It held opposing offenses to 183.6 yards per game, a total no defense has come close to matching since. The great Georgia defense of 2021, which earned such rave reviews, gave up a full two points more per game than the historic Alabama defense of a decade before.

Dont'a Hightower and Courtney Upshaw led the way, but there was plenty of dominance to go around. Dre Kirkpatrick stalked wide receivers at cornerback and Mark Barron patrolled at safety. C. J. Mosley was at linebacker too. That defense gave up just three rushing touchdowns all season.

It was the year of the Game of the Century, a 9–6 overtime loss to LSU before the rematch in the Superdome, a 21–0 Alabama win for Saban's second national championship at Alabama.

Trent Richardson was the running back and the main offensive weapon. When Richardson rushed for a 34-yard touchdown in the fourth quarter, it was the only touchdown scored in more than 60 minutes. AJ McCarron was a first-year starter who got better and better and then did just enough through the air against that remarkable LSU defense to help the Crimson Tide control the field position.

The only team that successfully ran on the Tide all season was Georgia Southern, a game that years later led to the famous Saban tin horn rant. The Eagles ran for 302 yards, 32 percent of the total allowed by Alabama's defense that season. Such was the dominance of that run-stuffing unit.

It was the second national title in three years for Saban and the Crimson Tide. A lesson had been learned in 2010, a three-loss team even with all that talent, and the 2011 team set the tone for what was to come the following season.

It was a team of good leaders, including Barrett Jones, Hightower, William Vlachos, Nico Johnson, and Josh Chapman. Most of that leadership returned for the 2012 team, and as already discussed, that led to some outstanding results and the without-a-doubt dynasty. That dynasty has continued, but the 2011 and 2012 teams are the only teams to win back-to-back championships since the mid-1990s.

"This team was a special team, not that the 2009 team was any different," Saban said. "And certainly an honor and a privilege to be with a group that sort of, I don't know, made the kind of commitment that you look for from a competitive character standpoint and intangibles that you always strive to try to get as a coach in a group, whether it's togetherness, the positive attitude, the responsibility and accountability they took for each other and themselves, and the hard work and discipline that went into...the development of this team. It was a really special group. And I feel very privileged to have been a part of that."

No. 6: 2017

This is a spot where I debated between two teams—the 2017 group and the team that followed in 2018. The 2018 team was an offensive juggernaut, breezing through the regular season before experiencing a bumpy road in the postseason.

Meanwhile the 2017 wasn't the same unit offensively, but it ultimately won the championship. When it came down to it, I valued the national championship more. That line of thought doesn't always hold (see: No. 7 and No. 8), but I made my choice and I have to live with it.

In all seriousness, this team will forever be known as the second-and-26 team. But there was so much more to the season that led up to that point, including a quarterback controversy, a top-ranked defense, injuries at linebacker and a roller-coaster regular season. That top-ranked defense is the last Alabama unit to rank No. 1 in total defense, what was then a regular occurrence in the Saban era. In the years that have followed, the defense consistently slipped each season up until 2021, when the unit climbed back into the top 10.

The regular season started with a much-hyped opener against Florida State in Atlanta, but that game was a dud and did not live up to the billing, as the Seminoles managed only seven points and lost their starting quarterback to a season-ending injury. A few weeks later UA beat down a 3–0 Vanderbilt team in Nashville, racking up 496 yards on the ground. The team got on a roll after that and then was somewhat tested against Texas A&M and LSU. And then came Mississippi State. The linebacker injuries really showed themselves against the Bulldogs, and the Crimson Tide found itself down seven points in the second half. A missed field goal to go ahead with around two minutes remaining gave Mississippi State the ball with a chance to win, but the UA defense forced a three-and-out. That's when a freshman wide receiver by the name of DeVonta Smith caught the game-winning touchdown with less than 30 seconds remaining.

But that game showed cracks in the nation's No. 1 team. Two weeks later the cracks broke wide open as Auburn controlled the Iron Bowl from start to finish in a 12-point win that seemed to end the Crimson Tide's season. But Auburn's loss to Georgia the following week opened the door again and Alabama got into the College Football Playoff as the No. 4 seed. Matching up against top-ranked Clemson for the third consecutive season, UA dominated the Tigers in a 24–6 win to advance Alabama to the national championship game for the third straight season. Alabama faced Georgia and, well, you know, second-and-26 became one of the most famous plays in college football history and introduced the sporting world to a freshman quarterback by the name of Tua Tagovailoa.

Saban was heralded for his coaching, making the decision to change quarterback from Jalen Hurts to Tagovailoa. "I felt like we've had this in our mind that, if we were struggling offensively, we would give Tua an opportunity, even in the last game," Saban said. "No disrespect to Jalen, but the real thought was, you know, they came into the game thinking we were going to run the ball and be able to run quarterback runs, which we made a couple of explosive plays on. But with the absence of a passing game and being able to make explosive plays and being able to convert on third down, I just didn't feel we could run the ball well enough, and I thought Tua would give us a better chance and a spark, which he certainly did. I couldn't be prouder of him [for] taking advantage of the opportunity. We have total confidence in him. We played him a lot in a lot of games this year, and he did very well. He certainly did a great job tonight."

No. 7: 2018

Tua mania took over this particular season. How could it not? Almost overnight the Alabama offense took off from a run-first unit to one that could score in the blink of an eye.

Quarterback Tua Tagovailoa, who'd been thrust into the spotlight given his heroic performance in the second half of the national championship game the season before, was the new starter, and he hit the ground running. Those receivers who came in with him in his recruiting class, a group affectionately known as the Ryde Outs, were right there with him and, along with freshman wide receiver Jaylen Waddle, formed one of the greatest wide-receiving units the game has ever seen. Jerry Jeudy, Henry Ruggs III, and DeVonta Smith with Waddle were nearly unstoppable.

Tagovailoa threw for nearly 4,000 yards, completing 69 percent of his passes for a touchdown-to-interception ratio of 43-to-6. Tua fever grew from week to week. The beatdowns were administered indiscriminately. In the first six games of the season, Alabama averaged 56 points a game. For the season, the team scored 92 touchdowns.

The difficulty in ranking these teams is applying a methodology that's consistent. For instance, if this team had won a national championship, I would have ranked it above the 2017 team (and I had a good debate with myself about putting it above 2011 as well). Certainly the 2018 team had an offense that could've outscored the 2017 group, but the 2017 defense was pretty stout. You get the picture. Winning a championship has to count for something, but how much? I have to call myself out because I haven't applied that methodology evenly. I have the 2018 team above the 2015 team, which did win a national championship. So methodology sees that I account for titles, and that's a large part of it, but it's not the be-all and end-all. There's a sort of feel to this too. And the feeling I get is that the 2018 team would beat the 2015 team head-to-head.

This team could've ended my internal debate if it had closed the deal in the national championship game against Clemson.

However, Alabama was run off the field in perhaps the most bizarre loss of Nick Saban's career. The Crimson Tide ran one of the worst fake field goals ever designed in this game. The weird part of the game is that Alabama moved the football, but they froze in the red zone and couldn't score. It's the worst loss, score-wise, of Saban's career at Alabama.

"First of all, you've got to give Clemson a little bit of credit," Saban said. "They have a really good team. I think the responsibility for us not playing well really starts with me. I thought the players prepared well for this game, and I think that they just got outperformed. It wasn't like we just didn't cover a guy. I mean, we tried to cover No. 8 [Justyn Ross]. He caught the ball, made a big play. We were in three-deep zone when No. 5 [Tee Higgins] [caught] a ball and [ran] 50 yards, 60 yards for a touchdown.... So you know, those responsibilities start with me, our staff, and all the coaches who try to get these guys ready, and when we don't play well, I feel like that's a reflection on the job that we did, the job that I did."

No. 8: 2015

This team was the one that inspired a hundred "Is the Alabama dynasty dead?" columns after the Crimson Tide was defeated by Ole Miss early in the season. Those concerns weren't well founded, it turns out, but it did seem something was off during this season. That loss to Ole Miss was in a game when Alabama started a new quarterback in Cooper Bateman. It was the only game he started in his UA career. Alabama turned the ball over five times and still had a chance to win the game at the end of the fourth quarter.

So off that performance, things looked uncharacteristically unsound, unlike Alabama football we'd seen up to that point. So it wasn't out of left field that some asked if the Alabama dynasty was dead. But they were wrong.

The week after the Ole Miss loss, Alabama hammered Georgia on the road and things started to right themselves. There was a scare against Tennessee that required some late heroics from quarterback Jake Coker and the top-ranked defense, but they managed to extend the winning streak over the Volunteers.

This team also played a classic national championship game against Clemson. Deshaun Watson gave a great Alabama defense fits with his combination of throwing and running. UA trailed heading into what would turn out to be a wild fourth quarter. Twenty-four of the Crimson Tide's 45 points occurred in the final 15 minutes. There was a touchdown pass to a wide-open O. J. Howard. There was a successful onside kick. There was a kickoff return for a touchdown by Kenyan Drake, and there was a recovery of an onside kick to melt the remaining time in the game away. There were some stressful minutes in that fourth quarter, but it led to an exciting game.

For a game with a back-and-forth quarter and all its scoring, it was the onside kick that captured the imagination. Saban called for it in the fourth quarter with the game tied. It was a shocking move. But not for Saban. "I made the decision to do it because the score was [24–24] and we were tired on defense and weren't doing a great job of getting them stopped, and I felt like if we didn't do something or take a chance to change the momentum of the game, we wouldn't have a chance to win," Saban said. "Getting that onside kick, I think, did change the momentum of the game. We scored on the big play two plays later, and then we had a kickoff return for a touchdown too, which was huge. So special teams was really big for us in this game."

No. 9: 2013

The one that got away. You could say that about the 2016 and 2018 seasons, but it most applies to the 2013 season. This was an experienced group that was a balanced team. It could play good offense and defense. It had leadership on both sides of the ball. The team went unbeaten all the way to the regular-season finale against Auburn. I don't need to tell you any more because it's likely a nightmare you've relived over and over. But it took one of the crazier games in the sport's history to keep the Crimson Tide from playing for a chance to win a third straight national championship. It wasn't to be, and the Kick Six ended that possibility, which is why it's accurate to call this season the one that got away.

AJ McCarron was an experienced quarterback who was getting his fair share of attention. He was even a Heisman Trophy finalist this season, finishing second. C. J. Mosley was the leader on defense, and he was the SEC Defensive Player of the Year and the Butkus Award winner. It was a great team, which makes the loss to Auburn all the more painful in retrospect.

It also makes one of the best plays in the history of this epic series become almost forgotten. The game was tied in the fourth quarter, and Alabama had the ball on its own 1-yard line. McCarron's 99-yard touchdown pass to Amari Cooper gave the Crimson Tide a seven-point lead and was a Heisman moment for McCarron. The lead didn't hold up because of Alabama's continued missed opportunities in the fourth quarter, including missed field goals, getting stopped on fourth-and-short, and a key holding call on O. J. Howard late in the game.

That all set the stage for one of the most dramatic game endings in college football history. It's one of the most what-could-have-been moments in recent history. "It was a great game," McCarron said. "Sometimes luck just isn't on your side. It's one of those crazy plays. It's almost like a video game. That's something you do on *Madden* or *NCAA*. It's just a wild play."

It's the most shocked I've seen Nick Saban after a game. It took a while for him to come to the postgame press conference. You could see him second-guessing himself and the decision to kick the field goal. He's not to blame, though. No one could have foreseen the ending playing out that way.

"We told our team that this is like March Madness," Saban said. "Coming into this game, [we told them] that if [they wanted] to keep playing in the tournament, [they had] to keep winning. I was really proud of the way our guys competed out there today, but the fact of the matter is that we did not make plays when we needed to."

No. 10: 2019

It was a somewhat weird year. Alabama offensively just bludgeoned opponents with Tua Tagovailoa at quarterback. Scoring never seemed to be the issue during this period of UA football. But the defensive slip continued this season, and the statistics back that up. Just two seasons earlier, the Crimson Tide ranked No. 1 in total defense. This season that ranking fell to No. 21, which is still a relatively good defense. But Alabama had never had to deal with "relatively good" under Saban. There was one thing you could consistently count on under Saban: that the defense would be great year in and year out no matter what personnel they lost. But that was no longer the case after Kirby Smart and Jeremy Pruitt were no longer the defensive coordinators. So Alabama had to outscore the great teams.

That's where the game of the year comes into play. That LSU team could put up points in a hurry, and it was easy to see why. Joe Burrow was the quarterback. Jordan Jefferson and Ja'Marr

Chase were the wide receivers. Clyde Edwards-Helaire was the running back behind a Joe Moore Award–winning offensive line. The Crimson Tide wasn't going to be able to shut them down, so it was up to the offense to outscore them. They came close.

With a somewhat hobbled Tagovailoa, who was dealing with an ankle injury, UA fell four points short in the defining game of the season. The Tigers went on to win the national championship.

The key sequence happened before the end of the first half. In the final 4:30 the game went from 16–13 to 33–13. Alabama fought back to pull within one score on multiple occasions in the second half, but LSU's offense was too good, making every play when it needed to. "We don't really control our own destiny, but if we finish the season the right way, we can see where it takes us," Saban said.

Unfortunately Alabama never got a chance to see where it would take them, as Tagovailoa sustained a gruesome hip injury in the next game against Mississippi State. Tagovailoa was lost for the season and never played for Alabama again, opting to go professional after his junior season.

The opportunity was there in the regular-season finale against Auburn with backup Mac Jones, but a couple of pick-six interceptions and a late missed field goal spoiled any chance for the Crimson Tide to backdoor their way into the College Football Playoff.

UA closed the season with a win over Michigan. There exists a feeling, though, that the talent was there to accomplish more than it did. Injuries and a sliding defense prevented that.

No. 11: 2008

It feels wrong ranking this team so low, but when compared against other Saban teams, the ranking seems justified. This was the team that returned Alabama football to prominence. They were the standard setters that other teams followed, which ultimately resulted in success. It was not the most talented team, but young talent from that team helped the next year's team to a championship. There were some lessons learned from the 2008 group that helped nudge the team in that direction.

In many ways, the 2008 unit overachieved. It had a legendary recruiting class, but those guys were all freshmen (including Mark Ingram and Julio Jones, among others). John Parker Wilson was the quarterback on the team, which went unbeaten up until the SEC Championship Game against the eventual national champion Florida Gators.

There were some great wins that season, starting with the season opener against Clemson, which served notice to the rest of college football that Alabama was no longer walking in the wilderness. They'd found a coach who knew how to build a program, and the Tigers found out the hard way. Georgia was the next team put on notice. The Bulldogs had won in overtime the season before in Tuscaloosa, but UA quickly let those in attendance know that it was no longer 2007. They raced out to a big lead quickly and led 31–0 at the half. The college football world was shocked. Saban tried to tamp down expectations. He didn't want anyone trumpeting this team as a championship contender. "After five games?" Saban said. "Let's see when we get a full body of work at the end of the season. It doesn't matter now. It doesn't matter until the end. We have a lot of good football teams ahead of us."

The LSU win on the road at Baton Rouge was an overtime special that was meaningful due to it being Saban's first game back in Baton Rouge since he departed LSU for the Miami Dolphins. But no game was as special to Alabama fans as the one that broke the streak. Auburn was riding a six-game winning streak over the Crimson Tide when it came in unranked and 5–6 in what would be Tommy Tuberville's last season. Alabama was No. 1 and 11–0. The dam was going to break. The Crimson Tide unleashed six years of pent-up frustration in a 36–0 win. By the end of the game, there was a light fog that hung over Bryant-Denny Stadium. After the game, the Million Dollar Band led a long rendition of "Rammer Jammer." It seemed to go into the night.

No. 12: 2010

The first team that underperformed is this group, a talented group but one that lacked focus and the ability to buy in to the Process coming off the national championship the season before. After this season, four Alabama players were drafted in the first round of the 2011 NFL Draft: Marcell Dareus, Julio Jones, James Carpenter, and Mark Ingram. But even with that elite talent, the Crimson Tide lost three games.

After holding off a pesky Arkansas team on the road, the Crimson Tide had its 19-game winning steak snapped at South Carolina. It's become one of the great trivia questions in recent college football history: "Who's the quarterback who beat Alabama to break the streak?" The answer is Stephen Garcia, and it was one of the highlight wins of Steve Spurrier's South Carolina career.

It was a loss you could almost sense that Saban saw coming. After the game he didn't mince words. "It's not like we just lost. They beat us," Saban said. "They out-executed us. They played better than we played. They played with more intensity. They played physical."

If the losses had stopped there, it would be one thing. But there was the road loss to LSU and a painful loss to Auburn in Tuscaloosa in a game Alabama led by more than three touchdowns until Auburn rallied. That loss was made more hurtful to Crimson Tide fans when Auburn went on to win the national championship. "We didn't finish the game," Saban said. "When you play good teams, you've got to play for 60 minutes. Those kinds of teams don't go away. There are a lot of lessons to be learned out there about finishing games and doing things correctly."

It is the last season in which Alabama lost three or more games. It seems like a wasted season, but it served as a teaching moment for the guys coming back for the 2011 team.

The season did end on a good note in the Capital One Bowl against the Michigan State Spartans. Alabama put a physical beating on the Spartans that those in attendance will never forget. It was as uncomfortable as I've ever been watching a team literally pummel the other team. It was the last time we ever saw Julio Jones, Mark Ingram, and Marcell Dareus in a Crimson Tide uniform, and they made sure it was memorable.

No. 13: 2021

The fact that this team won a SEC title and made it to the national championship game is a feather in the cap of Nick Saban. Kirby Smart, the coach of the Georgia team that beat Alabama for the national title, said that and more after the game. "I have a tremendous amount of respect for [Saban], the way he runs his program," Smart said. "And [this was] really probably one of the best jobs he's ever done with his team, because they were really young at some positions. And I think they've got the best player in college football in Bryce Young, and I saw it firsthand on the field in the SEC championship. But to do what he did this year, with that team, I told him after the game, I said, 'I really believe that this was probably the best job you've ever done.' And people don't understand that. Media don't respect that because they didn't win the national championship. But the job he did with that team? Incredible. Incredible."

This was one of the more inconsistent teams Saban has had. They were undisciplined and committed a lot of penalties. The offensive line was a shell of its former self, subjecting the quarterback to some hits he wouldn't normally have taken. The running game wasn't the same in short-yardage situations either.

But there were positives. The defense bounced back after three consecutive seasons of continuing to slip. The run defense was one of the best in the country, as was the pass rush. That was due to Will Anderson, the best defensive player in the country. Anderson won the Bronko Nagurski Trophy. He had 34.5 tackles for loss and 17.5 sacks. He was a menace for other teams to deal with.

The other positive was that the team had the best quarterback in college football. Bryce Young was the team's most valuable player, and he deservedly won the Heisman Trophy, the first quarterback in program history to do so.

Even with all the inconsistencies, the team beat undefeated No. 1 Georgia in the SEC Championship Game. No, they didn't just *beat* the Bulldogs; they *dominated* them. "I think what these guys really wanted to gain was more respect," Saban said. "Not just the fact that they were underdogs, because I think we had a tremendous amount of respect for Georgia, their team, and what they accomplished. But you guys gave us a lot of really positive rat poison. The rat poison that you usually give us is usually fatal, but the rat poison that you put out there this week was yummy."

No. 14: 2014

How good has the Nick Saban era been? There's a thousand different metrics that tell you the same story over and over again, but here's one of them. The team I rank next-to-last in the Saban era was the No. 1–ranked team in the inaugural College Football Playoff. So either I'm really bad at ranking teams (which could absolutely be true) or Saban is so good that even his "bad" teams are still elite.

It's a season known for Blake Sims and Amari Cooper on offense, and the pair had a magical connection all season. It was also Lane Kiffin's first season as the offensive coordinator. In many ways, this team overachieved. The quarterback was a converted running back. The defense was relatively slow at linebacker. It was caught not quite having adjusted to the spread and hurry-up, no-huddle. It showed. Still, the team lost only once during the regular season, at Ole Miss—to a spread hurry-up, no-huddle team no less—and won the SEC championship. In the first ever College Football Playoff, Alabama was the top seed.

That team lost in the Sugar Bowl to eventual national champion Ohio State, but it's a team that still won a championship. So why is it ranked No. 14? It's a legitimate question. My answer is I think the preceding teams would beat this particular team.

After the loss to the Buckeyes, a game which Alabama led 21–6 at one point, Saban did not concentrate on what was lost. "I think there's a lot of lessons to be learned from everything that was done here," Saban said. "I think some younger players get the opportunity to see what it takes to play well in big games, to prepare well for big games. I think there are a lot of lessons to be learned from your behavior and how you treat other people. This experience for our team is fantastic to come to the Sugar

Bowl and spend five days in the city of New Orleans. And these folks did a great job in terms of their hospitality. There are a lot of lessons to be learned when you have success, and there are also a lot of lessons to learn when you have failings, and hopefully we'll learn a lot from this experience and that will help us in the off-season. But I don't really think that we're going to change our philosophy in terms of how we do things. That philosophy has helped us win a lot of games, and hopefully it will continue to do the same thing in the future."

Alabama won the national championship the next season.

No. 15: 2007

Are you an Alabama superfan? Can you tell me what happened on the very first play from scrimmage during Nick Saban's first game as the Crimson Tide's coach? Don't cheat. If you answer "A 47-yard touchdown run by Terry Grant," you're correct. This team started with a bang, but the lack of talent and experience saw it end with a whimper.

The team started 6–2 and then lost its last four regular-season games to finish at 6–6. That outcome got the program invited to the Independence Bowl, where it outlasted Colorado to finish the season with a winning record.

There were high points to the season—starting a historic winning streak over Tennessee comes to mind—and there was the undoubtedly low point to the season and of the Saban era: the loss to Louisiana-Monroe. I was covering the game that day for the *Tuscaloosa News*. My assignment that day was to write a sidebar on the visiting team. Never did I think I'd be writing about the *winning* team. But the one thing I remember about that game above all others is senior linebacker Darren Mustin coming up for postgame interviews. He cried his eyes out. I remember how much that loss bothered him. For some reason that moment has stuck with me through the years.

Alabama, of course, upgraded the talent level in the following years, and the success followed. But that first team had some players who helped the program grow. Guys such as Rashad Johnson, Rolando McClain, Kareem Jackson, Javier Arenas, Lorenzo Washington, and Brandon Deaderick. As you can see, those guys set the foundation for the defense the next year, a team that got better, and several of those guys were there for the national championship year in 2009 too.

Greatness has to start somewhere; it has to have a foundation. That's what the 2007 group was: a starting point.

12

2020: The Greatest Team of All Time?

ALABAMA'S 2020 TEAM WAS THE PERFECT TEAM FOR AN imperfect season. Talent wasn't an issue, as evidenced by the six first-round draft picks in that spring's NFL Draft. The team had chemistry; the guys genuinely liked each other. It had leadership, helped by seniors who'd been around the block a few times. It had members willing to sacrifice social lives in a year of COVID. All of it added up to a perfect season against an all–Power 5 schedule.

If you're looking for a prime example of all those attributes rolled up into one player, consider Landon Dickerson.

Dickerson didn't get to play in the College Football Playoffs because he'd torn his ACL in the SEC Championship Game against Florida. It gutted his teammates. They gathered around him as the cart came on the field to take him to the locker room. He was the heart and soul of that team. A nasty center who played until the echo of the whistle, he was an easy fan favorite. He badly wanted to play in the national championship game. To the point that he came out in warm-ups fully dressed as if he were playing. He even snapped the ball to Mac Jones.

What no one knew but him was that he'd been working for an opportunity he didn't know would come. Until it did. With the clock running out, the senior center popped his helmet on and ran into the game, on a torn ACL, and took the final two snaps to clinch Alabama's 18th national championship.

In the days leading up to the national championship game, the Crimson Tide's affable yet tough-as-a-two-dollar-steak emotional leader would wake up and text his quarterback, Mac Jones, the same thing: "I'm playing, Mac. I'm playing." No one thought it possible because of his torn ACL. On his freshly reconstructed knee, he wanted to be there with his teammates, and he held onto a secret desire to take the final victory formation snaps to close out his career.

When Brian Robinson converted a third-and-9 deep in the fourth quarter with a 13-yard run, the entire sideline released a celebration meant for Dickerson, their permanent captain. They wouldn't have to punt. He would realize his dream. It was emotional. It was cathartic in a season like no other. Dickerson snapped the ball twice, and No. 1 Alabama (13–0) ran out the clock on a 52–24 blowout victory against No. 3 Ohio State in the College Football Playoff National Championship game inside Hard Rock Stadium.

Dickerson's teammates swarmed him with congratulatory hugs. Freshman wide receiver Javon Baker did backflips down the field. Jordan Battle, who'd been ejected for targeting in the first half, knelt and prayed, wiping tears from his eyes. Josh McMillon, who returned for his sixth year of eligibility, joined teammates to do snow angels in the confetti. They came back for exactly this: The confetti. The trophy. The smiles. The hugs. The tears. They came back for this moment, and to complete what they had started.

DeVonta Smith, Najee Harris, Alex Leatherwood, and Dylan Moses opted in for Alabama in the aftermath of a relatively disappointing end to the Crimson Tide's 2019 season, a win against Michigan in the Capital One Bowl. No offense to the fine folks in Orlando, but Alabama was accustomed to being in the College Football Playoff and had missed it for the first time in the event's history.

Those players made their decisions independently. Collectively, however, they sent a message: They began their Alabama careers with a national title in 2017, and they believed they could end their Alabama careers the same way in 2020. "The guys that did come back, I'm glad they came back," Smith said with a wry smile.

They had no idea how difficult it was going to be. But nothing worth having comes easily, and even through a pandemic, no spring practice, a stand for social justice, key injuries, the constant churn of COVID-19 testing and contact tracing, canceled games, and coaches missing games, their resolve was tested but never bested. Given the circumstances, the result was the most impressive individual season in Alabama history. A strong argument can be made that it's college football's greatest season of all time. The players weren't shy in staking their place in history. "I think we're the best team to ever play," Jones said. "There's no team that will ever play an SEC schedule like that again."

It started on December 31, 2019, with a social media post from Moses, who declared he was returning to Alabama to finish his business after an injury had cost him his junior season. That was followed by the now-infamous domino-falling GIF from the official Alabama football team Twitter. Though the team didn't get Tua Tagovailoa back, Smith, Leatherwood, and Harris reupping for another season formed the foundation of a record-setting offense.

Alabama doesn't often have a senior-laden team. That's just a side effect of recruiting elite athletes and developing those athletes to reach their potential. A specific set of circumstances helped get those juniors to come back to be seniors.

Smith hadn't been the biggest name in the wide-receiving corps with Jerry Jeudy, Henry Ruggs III, and Jaylen Waddle. Leatherwood wasn't as consistent as he wanted to be as a junior. With a tackle-heavy NFL Draft, he made the business decision to come back, round out his game, and increase his value for 2021. Harris was viewed as a good running back, but his choice to return paid dividends after the senior season he had. Perhaps his receiving ability improved his value the most; he became an every-down running back.

Smith, Leatherwood, and Harris never got a chance to set the tone in the off-season because the rug was pulled out from under them when spring practice was canceled in the SEC before it even started because of COVID-19. The pandemic ravaged the sports calendar and essentially every area of life, including how college classes would be held.

It wasn't a given there would even *be* a 2020 college football season. For a brief moment, when other conferences canceled their schedules in August, it appeared those players might have come back for nothing. But when the SEC announced it would play, the Crimson Tide were ready.

Nick Saban has said many times that this team holds a special place in his heart for myriad reasons, including the senior leadership, the overall closeness of the team, and the mutual respect the teammates had for each other and their coach. Saban told the players he loved them on more than one occasion. "Well, to me, this team accomplished more than any team," Saban said. "No disrespect to any other teams that we had or any championship teams. But this team won 11 SEC games. No other team has done that. They won the SEC, went undefeated in the SEC, then they beat two great teams in the playoff with no break in between.

"This is our fifth game in a row, from LSU to Arkansas to Florida to Notre Dame to here. Played 13 games, went undefeated with all the disruption that we had in this season. I think there's quite a bit to write about when it comes to the legacy of [this] team."

Saban earned the team's trust in the summer of 2020. That might be odd to read about the legendary coach, who earned respect from almost everyone a long time ago. But each team is its own organism.

One special way Saban bonded with this team was by supporting, and participating in, a message of social justice penned by Leatherwood. Leatherwood is not known as a particularly loquacious player, but when he wrote the words that later became a script for a video posted on Alabama's social media accounts, his message connected with the team. It was a message of unity, of overcoming racial injustice, and of striving for a better future for all people. Members of the team read those words, including Saban, who at one point read: "In this moment in history, we can't be silent. We must speak up."

Later in the summer, Saban and the team held a march from the football facility to historic Foster Auditorium, where the infamous Stand in the Schoolhouse Door —one of the seminal moments of the civil rights movement—took place on the

Alabama campus. Saban saw how important the message was to his team and stood out front during the march.

That Leatherwood would light the match that kicked all this off speaks to the leadership and the chemistry of this team. "I feel like it was important because I'm not a man of that many words, but I just felt like my voice needed to be heard because I'm more than just a football player," Leatherwood said. "I actually care about what goes on outside of this place. It was just super important for me to get my word across because it could impact a lot of people."

As the college football season closed in around it, the SEC remained firm that it would play a season. It would just look different. For Alabama, that meant instead of opening the season against traditional power USC in Texas, it began its quest on the road against Missouri. The Tigers had a first-year coach and didn't inspire much motivation as compared to the Trojans.

Still, the all-SEC schedule would be a different challenge than a normal Crimson Tide slate, which usually featured a prominent Power 5 opponent at a neutral site followed by three home nonconference games. In 2020 that would have been games against Georgia State, Kent State, and UT Martin. Instead Alabama got Missouri, Texas A&M, Ole Miss, Georgia, Tennessee, Mississippi State, LSU, Kentucky, Auburn, and Arkansas. Throw in Florida in the SEC Championship Game, and the only two conference opponents Alabama *didn't* end up playing were South Carolina and Vanderbilt.

Alabama sliced through that schedule like a hot knife through butter, which speaks to this team's place in history. In 13 games against only Power 5 competition (11 conference games, plus Notre Dame and Ohio State in the playoff), the average score was 49–19. Alabama beat teams ranked No. 2, No. 4,

No. 5, No. 7, and No. 13 in the final AP poll by an average of 19 points. In those games, it scored at least 40 points four times, including three games in the 50s. It did so with a passing attack that somehow didn't miss a beat after losing four first-round draft picks from the 2019 team (Tagovailoa, Ruggs, Jeudy, and Jedrick Wills Jr.). Alabama's scoring average and passing yards per game increased, even against a more difficult schedule.

Despite how flashy it came together on the field with explosive play after explosive play, the key cogs of this team weren't look-at-me guys. That extended to defense, where the SEC Defensive Player of the Year, Patrick Surtain II, was a quiet star. But the 2020 team began with the offense. From Jones to Smith to Harris to Leatherwood, it was a group of humble playmakers. "We have a great play caller, and then we have a great offensive line and skill players that make it all happen," Jones said that season.

Regardless of the topic, one word repeatedly came up to describe this Alabama team: *maturity*. They handled each thing that came their way—COVID-19 and related daily tests, injuries, distractions, egos, and more—as just another obstacle to overcome.

That applies to the distribution of the offense. Harris never upset the apple cart when he didn't get as many carries as he wanted, and none of the receivers begrudged another when their number was called. That helped offensive coordinator Steve Sarkisian just call football instead of massaging egos. "I think the one thing that this group is very unique at is... they play with one another, they play for one another, they celebrate one another with the successes they have because they recognize that is team success," Sarkisian said at the time. "The maturity on this team is really high. Through a year when all of us—coaches, players, different teams, professional sports, college sports—have dealt with a lot with the pandemic, our leadership on our team has been tremendous, and they've remained focused. They remained detailed in their approach. The result is we've played at a high level this year."

Dealing with COVID was obviously at the forefront. It was a seemingly never-ending fight to remain vigilant to keep the players and staff healthy, which required daily testing—an uncomfortable yet necessary experiment to ensure that no one was needlessly put at risk. The testing came at much expense to an athletic department in a shortened season and with reduced income because of a limited number of fans allowed in stadiums.

The team experienced numerous personnel disruptions as well, the most prominent of which involved Saban himself— twice. The head coach tested positive for COVID-19 before the Georgia game and missed most of the week before more tests revealed it was a false positive. On the day of the game, he tested negative and coached a decisive win against the Bulldogs. Saban tested positive again in November and missed the Iron Bowl against Auburn, watching from home as Sarkisian assumed coaching duties. "I think I did yell at the TV a couple of times. I guess it was more than a couple," Saban said following the game.

Just like every other bump during the season, the players cleared the hurdle and made it look easy. They did so despite losing two valuable members of the offense. When Jaylen Waddle went down in the fifth game of the season against Tennessee, DeVonta Smith became even more productive on his way to becoming the first wide receiver to win the Heisman Trophy since 1991. In the eight games after Waddle's injury, Smith averaged 162.5 yards and 2.4 touchdowns per game.

He saved his best for last. Despite dislocating a finger and missing most of the second half, Smith was uncoverable. He burned the Ohio State defense to the tune of 12 catches for 215 yards and 3 touchdowns. He was so dominant that his season totals of 1,856 yards receiving and 23 receiving touchdowns are better than the past two Heisman Trophy–winning wide receivers combined. (Tim Brown (1987) and Desmond Howard (1991) totaled 1,831 yards and 22 receiving touchdowns.)

Waddle gave the team an emotional boost against Ohio State, playing more snaps than originally thought in his return. He caught three passes for 34 yards and was on the field a lot when Smith was sidelined in the second half.

The team rose to the challenge of losing Dickerson, an emotional leader, to a serious knee injury for all but the final snaps of the playoff. The team also endured a postponed game when LSU dealt with COVID-19 issues. Through it all, not one Alabama player publicly opted out of the season. And the records fell game after game. Smith became the SEC's career leader in receiving yards, and Harris broke Derrick Henry's mark for most touchdowns in a season. Heck, even the kicker, Will Reichard, didn't miss a field goal or extra point all year.

Saban has won seven national championships, breaking the tie he shared with legendary Alabama coach Paul W. "Bear" Bryant. Many have pondered how much longer the 70-year-old Saban wants to continue the grind of coaching. If his disposition during the Auburn week is to be believed, Saban has lots of gas left in his tank. He was famously miserable missing the game. That's just who he is.

His accomplishments are many and varied. In 2021 he produced his fourth Heisman Trophy winner, tying him for second-most by a coach. He extended UA's record streak of being ranked No. 1 at some point in every season to 43 years. He's taken his teams to 10 national championship games, 9 with Alabama and 1 with LSU. And he's won seven of them.

He'll never say it, but a good argument can be made that the 2020 team represented Saban's best coaching job to date. To navigate the unknown, to keep his roster intact through it all while going unbeaten against an all–Power 5 schedule, was new territory for a coach who had already accomplished arguably as much as any coach in the history of the game.

Saban wasn't ready to have the conversation about his place in college football history or pulling ahead of Bryant's six national championships. After the game, he said, "I'm just happy that we won tonight, and I really haven't thought about [my legacy] because you're always looking forward, and I just love this team so much and what they've been able to do. I can't even put it into words."

Saban has won national championships in three different decades. His teams have morphed from defensive behemoths to offensive juggernauts. He is now 19–12 against AP top-three opponents; Bryant was 5–6. Every player from a Saban recruiting class at Alabama who has stuck around for four years has left with a national championship ring. The accolades stack up so deep that a mere list of them is inadequate.

Saban's place among the greats is cemented. His players don't doubt he's the greatest. "C'mon, man. Of course he is," Mac Jones said. "How could he not be? He does it the right way. He recruits well, but more importantly he develops great players and young men. I'm just so blessed that he gave me a chance to come here along with all my teammates. I wouldn't trade it for anything. He's the greatest to ever do it. He'll be the greatest for a long time."

And he's done it different ways, with an adaptable skill set he credited Bryant with having. Saban admitted that his 2020 team wasn't the same as the one the world saw in Miami eight years earlier against Notre Dame. That team won with a hulking defense, whereas the 2020 team was different. Saban embraced it. "We're an OK defensive team, not a great defensive team," Saban said. "We played well enough, got enough stops. But the offense was dynamic. That's what made the difference." The defense wasn't a classic Crimson Tide unit, but it held the Buckeyes to their second-lowest scoring output of the season. They forced five punts and turned OSU over on downs twice.

The 2020 season was a different kind of year for college football, and Alabama was a different kind of team. This team endeared itself to the fans in ways others hadn't. Maybe it was the pandemic, being stuck inside and isolated. Maybe it was the easy-to-love personalities of its best players—Smith, Dickerson, Harris, Jones, Leatherwood, and Surtain—that made it so easy to root for them.

Awards were handed out like Halloween candy, but the recipients didn't seem to care all that much. But they did care about the national championship trophy that Leatherwood passed around to as many players as he could reach.

This group came back for a national championship. Perhaps they didn't set out to make history, but that's exactly what they did. "In terms of legacy, I mean, I just think it's cool," Jones said. "Just the class that we had coming in, the four teams that I played on throughout my career here, I just am so blessed to be on each team. Two national championships—one kind of watching from the sideline, one getting a chance to play. It just goes to show that anything is possible. When you put your mind to something, believe in your teammates and coaches, you can get things done."

13

Legendary Recruits

Nick Saban will be the first to tell you that the secret to his success isn't his X's-and-O's acumen. There are a lot of coaches who can equal or surpass his ability in that arena. The secret to his success is that there is no secret to his success. Alabama has six national championships during his tenure because of the student-athletes he attracts to the Capstone.

There's a legend that upon his first visit to campus after accepting the job in 2007, Saban and then–director of athletics Mal Moore took a drive down University Boulevard in an SUV as Moore highlighted points of interest on campus. Moore was tickled that he'd landed the best college football coach in the country. In a moment of candor, Saban asked Moore if he really believed that he was the best coach in college football. Moore exclaimed in the affirmative, that he did believe that. Saban looked out the window and said, "I'm not the best coach, but I am the best recruiter." Such is the essence of Saban. He attracts the best of the best.

It's been said that Saban is so good at recruiting that he doesn't recruit—he *selects*. It's like he goes grocery shopping and selects what he wants. Top recruiting class after top recruiting class proves that he is among the best recruiters the game has ever seen. He's done it through multiple eras of college football—before social media; during social media; before name, image, and likeness; and after name, image, and likeness. No matter how the ground shifts underneath him, he finds his footing and thrives.

Thinking about the amount of talent he's brought in is staggering. He develops that talent too—46 of his players were drafted in the first round, including 41 from Alabama. It's the most first-rounders produced by a coach overall and at a single program. Following is a list of the players from Alabama drafted in the first round of the NFL Draft:

2009: **Andre Smith** (No. 6, Cincinnati)

2010: **Rolando McClain** (No. 8, Oakland), Kareem Jackson (No. 20, Houston)

2011: **Marcell Dareus** (No. 3, Buffalo), **Julio Jones** (No. 6, Atlanta), **James Carpenter** (No. 25, Seattle), **Mark Ingram** (No. 28, New Orleans)

2012: **Trent Richardson** (No. 3, Cleveland), **Mark Barron** (No. 7, Tampa Bay), **Dre Kirkpatrick** (No. 17, Cincinnati), **Dont'a Hightower** (No. 25, New England)

2013: **Dee Milliner** (No. 9, New York Jets), **Chance Warmack** (No. 10, Tennessee), **D. J. Fluker** (No. 11, San Diego)

2014: **C.J. Mosley** (No. 17, Baltimore), **Ha Ha Clinton-Dix** (No. 21, Green Bay)

2015: **Amari Cooper** (No. 4, Oakland)

2016: **Ryan Kelly** (No. 18, Indianapolis)

2017: **Marlon Humphrey** (No. 16, Baltimore), **Jonathan Allen** (No. 17, Washington), **O. J. Howard** (No. 19, Tampa Bay), **Reuben Foster** (No. 31, San Francisco)

2018: **Minkah Fitzpatrick** (No. 11, Miami), Daron Payne (No. 13, Washington), **Rashaan Evans** (No. 22, Tennessee), **Calvin Ridley** (No. 26, Atlanta)

2019: **Quinnen Williams** (No. 3, New York Jets), **Jonah Williams** (No. 11, Cincinnati), **Josh Jacobs** (No. 24, Oakland)

2020: **Tua Tagovailoa** (No. 5, Miami), **Jedrick Wills Jr.** (No. 10, Cleveland), **Henry Ruggs III** (No. 12, Las Vegas), **Jerry Jeudy** (No. 15, Denver)

2021: **Jaylen Waddle** (No. 6, Miami), **Patrick Surtain II**, (No. 9, Denver), **DeVonta Smith** (No. 10, Philadelphia), **Mac Jones**, (No. 15, New England), **Alex Leatherwood** (No. 17, Las Vegas), **Najee Harris** (No. 24, Pittsburgh).

2022: **Evan Neal** (No. 7, New York Giants), **Jameson Williams** (No. 12, Detroit)

There are other great recruits who have come through the program. What would a list of the top recruits looks like? Should it be solely based on when they were drafted? How about what they meant in their individual recruiting class? A mix of both? Based solely on collegiate results? Maybe all of the above?

Let's take a swing at some of the top recruits of the Saban era. Before we get started, I'll get a formality out of the way. These are in no particular order, and it's not meant to be an exhaustive list. Otherwise the list would be 100 players deep. So save your ire, because I know that Derrick Henry and several others should be on this list too. With that out of the way, here you go.

Julio Jones
Class of 2008
Five-Star Recruit

The 2008 recruiting class was Saban's first complete recruiting class after taking the job the previous January, and Jones was the cherry on top of what was already a great class. Jones didn't particularly like the recruiting process and remained pretty tight-lipped when he went to the Foley High School gymnasium to announce his choice. He was down to Alabama and Oklahoma, and there was a lot of nervousness in the UA football offices. But when Jones put on that Alabama hat, it sent the country a message that Alabama was once again going to be a program to reckon with. Alabama wasn't a team that threw the ball all over the field, and to beat out Oklahoma for a top-notch wide receiver was a big deal. Jones helped set the culture of Alabama football with an unmatched work ethic. He is truly the first big one Saban landed, and it helped set the stage for what was to come from Saban and the Crimson Tide.

"He was one of the most highly touted players at his position, and probably one of the best players in the country," Saban said. "Being from Alabama, it was probably one of the most important things that ever happened in the program. When Julio, Mark Barron, [Dont'a Hightower], all those guys came in the first class—there were probably six to seven first-round draft picks—they all came here when we weren't any good. We were coming off a 7–6 season, so they came here, and they believed. They trusted in what we were trying to do to create a program, and they wanted to prove something. There was nobody we had that was a better leader, or did more to enhance the culture of toughness and effort than Julio Jones did. He used to run down on kickoff and would not come off the kickoff team during the game. There were a lot of guys that made an impact in the early years, but Julio was the guy who led the way."

Dont'a Hightower
Class of 2008
Four-Star Recruit

Hightower was a member of Saban's first big recruiting class, which turned Alabama around. The 2008 class contained players such as Julio Jones and Barrett Jones. Hightower wasn't one of the bigger names of the class, but he was an immediate impact player. He started all 14 games in his freshman season. Then he suffered a severe knee injury that cost him most of his sophomore season. He returned in 2010, but he was still not 100 percent from the knee injury. It wasn't until the 2011 season that he fully returned and showed how disruptive he could be.

That season, he was the most valuable player for a defense that is considered one of the greatest in the history of college football. In 13 games in 2011, he had 85 tackles, including 11 tackles for loss and 4 sacks. He authored arguably the most memorable play in the national championship game against LSU when he strip-sacked Tigers quarterback Jordan Jefferson on fourth down.

Hightower hadn't been able to play in the national championship game against Texas during the 2009 season due to his injury. He made sure his first national championship game in 2011 was memorable. "Not playing in that [2009] game gives me a little more fire than I think everybody else," Hightower said at the time. "And I can definitely speak on our behalf and the whole defense that we're all going to go out and leave it all on the field."

He represents the throwback body type that defined the Alabama front seven for so long under Saban. Those Crimson

Tide defenses were bigger and stronger than most, and they completely shut down the run. That's why that Alabama team allowed fewer than 2.5 yards per carry and only three rushing touchdowns all season.

Hightower actually saw what was coming with the 2011 defense. He sort of predicted it. "I do feel like this is best defense I've been a part of," Hightower said. "I feel like we have exactly what it takes. It's all about how we go out and use it, how we take advantage of our resources we have, whether it be coaching, getting in with coaching, watching a little bit of film, or getting an extra workout. I feel like it's going to come down to that, because we have the right coaches and the right players. It's all about how we use them."

Those defenses defined Alabama for a long time, and Hightower was the face of how they wanted to play—a jumbo linebacker who could move well and pressure the quarterback. That's changed with the program going smaller to combat the spread and the hurry-up, no-huddle, but it doesn't change history.

Hightower made sure he left his impression on the program, literally. He was voted a permanent team captain by his teammates, meaning his hand- and footprints are forever enshrined at Denny Chimes on the quad. "It means a lot," Hightower said. "When you go to Denny Chimes and you look along the ground, you see some big names. It means a lot to me to have the opportunity to leave my stamp on the University of Alabama. It's real big. There's not a lot of places like Alabama when it comes to tradition, and that's one of the reasons I came here—the tradition. So it was a real big honor for me to be able to leave my stamp there at the University of Alabama."

Trent Richardson
Class of 2009
Five-Star Recruit

Nick Saban went head-to-head with defending national champion Florida and Urban Meyer in pursuit of Richardson, and although the player had been pledged to Alabama for some time, heading into national signing day, there were some rumors that Florida was trending. At Richardson's Pensacola high school, the anxiety built until he announced he was sticking with Alabama.

The Crimson Tide has had a parade of great running backs in the Saban era, and a couple of Heisman Trophy winners in Mark Ingram (2009) and Derrick Henry (2015), but when Richardson signed, none of that was true. To full comprehend why Richardson is on this list, you need to comprehend that when he came, Alabama wasn't the Alabama it is now. It had no national championships under Saban.

After signing with Alabama, Richardson told me: "It was hard telling Urban Meyer no with him sitting in my mom's living room with those rings on." Meyer had two national championship rings from Florida. Saban had none from Alabama. Securing his signature sent a message to Meyer that Saban and Alabama were for real and the 2008 recruiting class was no joke. Alabama would get its national championship that season, and Richardson played a major role with a pair of touchdown runs against Texas, including a 49-yarder. Florida has been a very fertile recruiting territory for Alabama under Saban.

Tua Tagovailoa
Class of 2017
Five-Star Recruit

Alabama had great quarterbacks before and after him, but he will be remembered as the first elite quarterback of the Saban era, the one who seemed to transcend the game with the flick of a wrist.

The program had long been thought of as a power-running offense, and it was, but Tagovailoa made the Crimson Tide the *it* offense in college football. He ushered in an era of explosiveness when you didn't dare take your eyes off the action for fear of missing an electrifying pass play. After coming off the bench to lead Alabama to a walk-off national title win as a freshman, Tagovailoa finished as the runner-up in the Heisman Trophy race as a sophomore.

"I can think back to four or five players and actually can say I really love those guys as people—the way they did things, the contribution that they made, how they affected other people—and Tua would be one of those four or five guys," Saban said. "I mean, he's just a fabulous person, a really good player, really cares about his team and his teammates, and I haven't had one issue or problem with him since he's been here. He's worked hard. He's supported his teammates when he didn't play. He supported Jalen [Hurts] when he didn't play. Jalen supported him when he didn't play. So I can't say enough good things about him and his family and the impact that they've had on the program."

Amari Cooper
Class of 2012
Four-Star Recruit

You didn't even need to see who made the catch. You could hear it: "Cooooop!" For three seasons "Coop" rang out across football fields throughout the southeast, as Cooper was nearly unstoppable. He'd been spotted at Alabama's summer camp, and that was the only evaluation that needed to be done. He was that impressive. He fit right in with a work ethic that all the great ones who've come to Alabama have. He was quiet and reserved and did his talking with the way he would outwork you. Once he got on campus, word quickly got out that UA had its next elite receiver. I remember getting a text message that summer that stated Cooper was the best wide receiver they'd had in camp since Julio Jones. That's a strong statement. It turned out to be true.

Playing with quarterback AJ McCarron, Cooper had an excellent freshman season, highlighted by his winning touchdown catch in the SEC Championship Game against Georgia. He won the Biletnikoff Award as a junior, given to the nation's best receiver, and was a Heisman Trophy finalist. He set school records in three years in the program, most of which just recently fell to Heisman winner DeVonta Smith. Cooper choosing Alabama led directly or indirectly to the pipeline of South Florida receivers traveling to Alabama. It also signaled that elite receivers could come to Alabama and be featured, something that had not happened previously to the level Cooper achieved.

Landon Collins
Class of 2012
Five-Star Recruit

Collins will be remembered as one of the first significant athletes Saban recruited from the state of Louisiana, from which it can be notoriously difficult to pull a player over state lines. He wasn't the first, but his commitment to Alabama over LSU, on live television, was one of the must-see moments in recruiting history. His mom's reaction sealed that with the public disapproval in her body language and in her words. Collins's recruitment also set the stage for Saban and staff to swoop in the next year and grab the top player in Louisiana again, this time left tackle Cam Robinson.

"We feel like Landon Collins is an outstanding player. He's a fine young man who was in our camps the last couple years," Saban said. "He has leadership qualities, he's a great competitor, he's a good student, [and] he's a very bright young guy who I feel is going to be very successful here."

Jonathan Allen
Class of 2013
Five-Star Recruit

The DMV area has been good to Alabama over the years, with players such as the Kouandjio brothers, Trevon Diggs, Cyrus Jones, Keilan Robinson, DeMarcco Hellams, Shane Lee, Chris Braswell, Darrian Dalcourt, and Monkell Goodwine. The DC metro area has quietly been one of the program's most fertile recruiting grounds. But no such recruit has been more important than Jonathan Allen. He was a difference maker on the Crimson Tide almost immediately. Allen's family military background was a perfect fit for Saban's famed Process. At Alabama he won nearly every defensive award one could win.

By the time he left, he'd won a national championship, SEC Defensive Player of the Year, the Bronko Nagurski Trophy, the Lombardi Award, and the Chuck Bednarik Award, and he was a unanimous All-American. Saban beat out the likes of Maryland, Michigan, and Florida for his services. Allen set the tone for arguably Alabama's best defense of the Saban era in 2016.

Rashaan Evans
Class of 2014
Five-Star Recruit

He was from Auburn. He went to Alabama. That says nearly everything there is to say about a player being his own man and doing what's best for him. It's not often that a player residing in your biggest rival's hometown, who is also a legacy to that program, chooses his own way. It was such a certainty that he was going to Auburn that it left the state in shock when he picked Alabama. It was truly an upset when Evans picked Alabama over Auburn, the program for which his father played. That didn't sit well at Auburn, and it remains controversial to this day. An online petition to boycott Evans's father's business spread across the Internet.

Evans went on to win two national championships with the Crimson Tide, so he got the last laugh. He chose Alabama over Auburn specifically because he and his family felt UA's system and how Evans would be used would be a better fit. With Evans's family remaining in the Auburn area, him choosing Alabama remained a storyline throughout his four years in Tuscaloosa. The Crimson Tide used his speed and bulked him up, and he was able to play both inside and outside linebacker during his time in the program.

Minkah Fitzpatrick
Class of 2015
Five-Star Recruit

Alabama had to hold off Florida State late in the recruitment process, and it's a good thing they did. The ability to play in Saban's secondary and the fact that Alabama put so many players in the league were the determining factors in Fitzpatrick's choice. He was headed for stardom from the moment he arrived in Tuscaloosa. Such was his talent and ability to maximize that talent with a work ethic that Saban praises.

A quiet superstar, Fitzpatrick came in and made his mark as a freshman while continuing the culture that players such as Julio Jones and Barrett Jones established. Fitzpatrick was like a coach on the field. He had the ability to play nearly all the spots in the secondary. In his three-year career, he was a two-time All-American and won the Bednarik and Jim Thorpe Awards.

When he opted for the NFL instead of a senior season, he put his decision to pick Alabama over Florida State into context. "The best three years of my life have been at the University of Alabama," he said. "Me and my family have been through a whole lot of highs and lows. We rebuilt our homes, rebuilt our lives, and centered our lives around Christ. We've accomplished a lot together, a lot of things that not many people can say they've accomplished as a family and as a unit. We've won two national championships together, and I've attended one of the greatest universities in the world."

Cam Robinson
Class of 2014
Five-Star Recruit

Getting No. 1 tackles in the country isn't a new thing to Alabama now, but it was relatively new to Alabama at the time, especially out-of-state offensive tackles. UA had done it with Cyrus Kouandjio in 2011, but landing Robinson was still a big deal, especially because he was from Louisiana. The number of five-star tackles from Alabama now reads off like a who's-who list. Guys such as Jonah Williams, Jedrick Wills, Alex Leatherwood, Evan Neal, JC Latham, and Tommy Brockermeyer. Alabama produces at offensive tackle, and Robinson is a big part of that legacy. Robinson won a national championship and was a three-time SEC champion. He won the Outland Trophy and the Jacobs Blocking Trophy and was a unanimous All-American.

"Cam's first of all an outstanding athlete," Saban said in the lead-up to Robinson's NFL Draft. "He can play left tackle or right tackle actually, in my opinion, but I think he'd be a fantastic left tackle. He's very athletic. He's got great length and size. Good pass protector. He can be physical when he needs to be in terms of getting movement on the run."

Barrett Jones
Class of 2008
Four-Star Recruit
Jones is arguably the most decorated player in program history, with a list of bona fides that reads like something out of a record book. He won three national championships starting at three different positions. He won the Outland Trophy. He won the Rimington Trophy. He was a freshman All-American guard. He was an All-American right tackle. He was an All-American center. He was a consensus All-American twice. Plus, he was a part of the class that is credited with bringing Crimson Tide football back to the forefront. Jones is the Process personified. He wasn't just a great football player on great teams. He was a model student, graduating with a degree in accounting with a 4.0 grade-point average. He was on the team's leadership

council. You get the point. When he arrived in 2008, he helped set the tone for what the program was to become. He left having succeeded in every way.

His versatility was a key to those Crimson Tide offensive lines. "Well, I think it tells you what kind of special person, competitor, and athlete Barrett Jones is," Saban said. "I was asked earlier today [if I] have...ever seen anybody else that could do these things sort of so effortlessly and consistently in terms of the performance level. I think it's because Barrett is bright, he's a very good athlete, and he's not affected by change like a lot of people would be.

"Probably the only offensive lineman that I've ever been associated with [who compares to Jones] was Bruce Matthews at the Houston Oilers. He could play center, he could play guard, he could play tackle, he was a long snapper. He's the only guy that I ever remember. That's pretty high-class there to be compared to someone like him.

"Barrett Jones has been an outstanding leader on our team on and off the field, and his academic record is absolutely as good as anybody we've ever been around."

Will Anderson
Class of 2020
Five-Star Recruit

Believe it or not, Anderson sort of flew under the radar in terms of high-visibility recruitments. His home-state program Georgia Bulldogs didn't see a place for him in Kirby Smart's defense, and Alabama was the beneficiary big time. Like those stars before him, it didn't take long for him to earn his standing on the team. Reports quickly surfaced that he was unblockable. He even quickly earned the nickname the Terminator. He obviously hasn't disappointed. He's widely viewed as the best defensive player in college football. Multiple scouts told me he'd be the No. 1 pick in the 2022 NFL Draft if he were draft eligible. He also possesses a likable personality and quickly welcomed leadership responsibilities even as a young player. He was voted a permanent team captain by his teammates as a sophomore.

"We loved Will Anderson in high school," Saban said. "He had great size; you could see the initial quickness, explosive power. We didn't know for sure if he'd end up being a stand-up player or end up playing down—he kind of does both for us now and does both very well. He's certainly been everything that we thought he would be, and I think that's because of the kind of person he is, the kind of competitive character he has, the leadership qualities that he has. The guy's always trying to get better."

Bryce Young
Class of 2020
Five-Star Recruit

When you win the program's fourth Heisman Trophy and become the first quarterback to do so, it's almost requisite that you be included on a list like this. Alabama beating out USC for him, especially in their own backyard, was notable.

He lived up to his billing as a five-star prospect when he won the opportunity to start as a sophomore. He led the team to an SEC title and a national championship game appearance. He played with the standard that Saban set in the recruiting process. Even in the loss to Georgia in the national championship game, Saban made sure he let everyone know what Young meant to the team in 2021 when he singled out Young and his teammate Will Anderson for their efforts during the season.

"He's an easy guy to coach," Saban said. "He tries to do everything the right way. He wants to do everything the right way. He always prepares well for the game. He's got a great personality. He's got really good leadership qualities about him."

DeVonta Smith
Class of 2017
Four-Star Recruit
With a résumé like Smitty's, do I even need to write why he is significant? From catching second-and-26 to the five touchdown catches against Ole Miss in 2019 to winning the Heisman Trophy his senior season, Smith had a storybook career at Alabama. How many players dream of a walk-off touchdown in the national championship game? He lived it. Then he stuck around for three more seasons to rewrite the Alabama receiving record book. He even had a nickname too: the Slim Reaper. It's fitting given his physical stature, but he played anything but slight.

Saban even poked fun at those who continued to bring up his size during the draft process. "To look at him and say he only weighs 170 pounds as a reason not to pick him, I would say to them: 'The ball weighs 13 ounces. How big do you have to be to carry it?' I would first off have to say that I think his performance speaks for itself," Saban said. "I'll be honest with you, when we recruited DeVonta Smith, he weighed 159 pounds. I wished he was bigger. And now he weighs 170 pounds and I think people at the next level are probably saying, 'I wish he was bigger.' But...there are bigger people who don't perform anywhere near how he performs. There are people that are bigger than him that don't have the competitive spirit that he has or the competitive toughness."

14

2017: Recruiting the Best

THE LIFEBLOOD OF ANY COLLEGE PROGRAM LIES IN ITS recruiting. Coaches set the tone, form a philosophy, develop athletes once they arrive on campus, and are responsible for translating all of that into wins on the field. But they have to attract the talent first.

That's never been a problem for Nick Saban, one of the greatest recruiters in the sport's history. He's compiled several legendary classes in his time as the head coach of the Crimson Tide. The 2008 group was the first big one. They are ones who started getting the program headed to where it is today. Guys such as Mark Ingram, Julio Jones, Barrett Jones, Mark Barron, and Dont'a Hightower are the reasons Saban was able to turn Alabama around so quickly and move them from 7–6 in his first year to 12–2 in his second year and finally to 14–0 national champions in his third year.

There were other great recruiting classes along the way, and every member of every one of his recruiting classes won a national championship if he stayed in the program. But no class matches the 2017 group in terms of sheer talent. That group included six five-star players in the 247Sports composite rankings: Najee Harris, Tua Tagovailoa, Alex Leatherwood, Dylan Moses, Jerry Jeudy, and LaBryan Ray. It included four players who finished in the top five in Heisman Trophy voting at some point in their career: Tagovailoa was a finalist in 2018, and DeVonta Smith won it in 2020, and Mac Jones and Harris also appeared in the top five of voting. The class included almost every major individual award the sport gives out. There were an astounding eight first-round NFL draft picks: Tua Tagovailoa, Mac Jones, Najee Harris, Jaylen Waddle, DeVonta Smith, Jerry Jeudy, Henry Ruggs III, and Jedrick Wills Jr. Xavier McKinney was selected in the second round with the 36th overall pick; Isaiah Buggs was a sixth-round selection; and seven players, including Evan Neal, Jameson Williams, Phidarian Mathis, and Brian Robinson were selected in the 2022 draft. Five of the top 36 players drafted in 2020 were from Alabama's 2017 recruiting class. Simply put, that class is legendary.

How did that class come together? Well, that's the stuff of legend. When Najee Harris stepped onto the plane in San Antonio fresh from the U.S. Army All-American Bowl, bound for Birmingham with his good friend Tua Tagovailoa in tow, it ended the back-and-forth, Alabama-or-Michigan drama of where the top-ranked running back from California would go to school. Harris, though he had verbally pledged to Alabama, has admitted that up until the very last moment, he didn't know where he was going to go. He had plane *tickets*, plural—one to Alabama, the other to Michigan. He talked to Tagovailoa one last time, and then got on the plane bound for 'Bama.

That decision cemented Alabama's status as the No. 1 recruiting class in 2017, perhaps the all-time greatest in recruiting history. There are multiple ways to evaluate recruiting classes. One is in the moment, taking the rankings of each player and essentially adding up all the classes to see which one ranks higher. The other is to let it play out, to see what that collection of 25 or so players turns out to be. And no matter which standard you apply to the 2017 Alabama class, it wins. It won on paper on national signing day; it won on the field with all the class accomplished, including two national championships, four national championship game appearances (that's if you count the fifth-year guys that played in the 2022 CFP final), and two Heisman Trophy winners; and it won in the NFL draft.

When that class was fully signed and on campus in Tuscaloosa, one assistant coach on that Alabama staff, on the condition of anonymity, told me, "We should all be fired if we don't play for multiple national championships with this class." They weren't fired. Alabama played for a national championship in that class's freshman season and won it, did it again in its sophomore season but lost it, went again in its senior year and won it again, and those who stuck around for a fifth year played for it again, but lost. Simply stunning. But it goes to show that those talent evaluators knew what they had from the moment those players arrived. There are times in history when a collection of talent coalesces in such a way that expectations can't help but be affected. This was one of those times.

There are no guarantees, though—only educated guesses. Sometimes they're right. Sometimes they're wrong. You can't account for chemistry—the way a team comes together and if the players actually like each other. This class did. Instantly. You also can't predict injury, such as the way Tagovailoa's history with injuries affected individual games (the 2018 SEC Championship Game) and seasons (his 2019 season-ending injury against Mississippi State). But on the hoof, everyone in the program knew how good that collection of talent was, and it didn't take long to figure out. Sometimes you just know. That's the general feeling the Alabama coaching staff had when it signed the class of 2017. "Best class ever," then–offensive line coach Mario Cristobal told me.

Its curriculum vitae is unmatched by nearly any metric you wish to apply. The class started early with a dramatic walk-off victory in the national championship game as Tagovailoa connected with Smith for a 41-yard touchdown pass on second-and-26 in overtime. Winning the title that year, some freshmen from that class played key roles. Obviously Tagovailoa and Smith connected on the championship-winning touchdown, but Alex Leatherwood was protecting on that play, having been moved to left tackle during the game in place of an injured Jonah Williams. Najee Harris made key runs in the fourth quarter of that game. To win a national championship in their first year with several members of the class playing key roles in the title game only built the confidence of the class. It made them legends early on too.

Those players were blown out a year later in the title game, and the next year was derailed when Tagovailoa was injured. But the class went out on top in 2020 with truly one of the best teams of all time. "I look on that class a lot," said Leatherwood, the starting left tackle on that 2020 team. He won the Outland Trophy that season as the nation's best interior lineman, the sixth such award in the program's history. "I feel like we're the greatest [class] of all time if you ask me. We had a lot of talent.

But aside from us all being talented, things like that, we're all hard workers. And we all had a common goal in mind, and that was to win a national championship and be the best players that we could be. And that's why we came here."

Leatherwood played a large role in the first national title that class claimed, replacing injured Jonah Williams at left tackle in the second half of the title game. That was the first sign of how special that class was: how many players contributed to winning that national championship as freshmen. Aside from Leatherwood being forced into action, one of the most famous coaching decisions of all time involved Nick Saban benching Jalen Hurts, later a Heisman Trophy finalist at Oklahoma, for Tagovailoa, a true freshman.

When Saban opted for Tagovailoa to take the field in the second half, he opened himself up to immense criticism if the decision went sideways. Instead Alabama erased a 13–0 deficit and won 26–23 in overtime. It did so because of what Tagovailoa did. Again, the stuff of legends.

But the offense also heavily leaned on Harris in that game. Harris carried the ball only six times—all in the fourth quarter—but he averaged 10.7 yards per rush in a huge fourth quarter that set the stage for the dramatic.

Then there's the legend of "Mr. Second-and-26," Smith. He has grown tired of reliving that day and has made sure not to be represented by just one play. He finished his career as Alabama's leading receiver in almost every category. He caught five touchdowns in a single game against Ole Miss, and of course, he won the Heisman Trophy. But considering the magnitude of second-and-26, he'll always be remembered for that. That will never go away.

Neither will the bond of that class. "A lot of us, we went to a lot of camps together," Smith said. "We talked to each other.

Some of us kind of knew where others were leaning to and some of us were already kind of committed here. And it was just everybody recruiting each other, just building the relationship. And I feel like that's what made us so close: before we even got here, the relationships that we had. Just how close everybody was and everybody's dedication to this team, everybody wanting to come in and put in the work."

That so many players from that class—so much of the upper-shelf talent—stuck around for their senior seasons is a story in itself. Leatherwood was caught in a tackle-heavy class of draftable players his junior season in 2019. He also wanted to hone his game more. Smith wasn't the biggest wide receiver prospect in that recruiting class, and Jeudy and Henry Ruggs III were top-15 picks in 2019. Harris's return was truly a surprise. Much like with his recruitment, he was tight-lipped. And much like his recruitment, he made no announcement. He just showed up in Tuscaloosa again. At the end of the season, after beating Michigan in the Capital One Bowl, it was almost assured that Harris was gone. But he made no announcement, and his decision kind of hung up in the air. Then COVID hit and Harris wasn't on campus. There was no spring football, but when Saban and the athletic department established clear protocols for the players' safety, Harris returned. He was back in, and boy did it pay off in helping his draft stock. Had he left in 2019, he wasn't viewed as a first-round guy. After what he did in 2020, it was almost guaranteed. He went in the first round to the Pittsburgh Steelers.

Those three formed the foundation of Alabama's historic offense. Well, those three and Mac Jones, the three-star quarterback from that class whom no one knew much about prior to 2020. Jones, who originally committed to Kentucky, was once the odd man out behind Hurts and Tagovailoa. It certainly didn't end that way. All three ended up being Heisman Trophy finalists. Jones, who finished third in the 2020 Heisman voting, won the Davey O'Brien and Johnny Unitas Golden Arm Awards. That's not bad for a scrawny recruit who was an afterthought in the 2017 class behind Tagovailoa. He was almost the safety quarterback and viewed as a guy who would be a career backup.

He didn't view it that way, though. He had an unwavering belief in himself. "I knew they were all special, even before we got here at camps and stuff, all those guys—Smitty, Ruggs, Jeudy—throwing to them at camps [was] really cool opportunity," Jones said. "Obviously, you can look at that class [and] be like, 'Wow.' Right now, there's a few guys in the NFL, a few guys that will be in the NFL probably next year. And it's really cool to be part of that class. I was kind of the second quarterback. And obviously, I've learned from Tua and learned from everybody in that class. It's been really cool to be a part of that growth."

In one of the greatest stories of the 2020 season, Jones played his way into being a first-rounder, even as draft pundits and some college football analysts were incredulous at that thought. He proved the New England Patriots' belief in him was worth it by winning the starting job in the preseason. In the quarterback-heavy 2021 draft, Jones by far had the best season. That doesn't mean his career will end up being better than that of Trevor Lawrence or Justin Fields or Trey Lance or Zach Wilson; it just means the Patriots were correct in spending a first-round pick on the three-star quarterback from Alabama.

When Jones joined Smith, Harris, and Leatherwood, it cemented eight first-round draft picks from that 2017 Alabama recruiting class. Those UA assistants who put the class together knew what they were talking about. "We felt we would have the best roster in the country for the next four years," one former assistant said.

Cristobal was more succinct but just as firm in his analysis: "The best recruiting class of the Saban era."

Those are strong words, considering the 2008 recruiting class—headlined by Mark Ingram, Julio Jones, Mark Barron, Marcell Dareus, Barrett Jones, Dont'a Hightower, Terrence Cody, and Courtney Upshaw—has long held that title. There's now a feeling that the 2008 class turned the Crimson Tide program around and the 2017 class elevated it to unseen levels.

Saban doesn't deal in those arguments. He rarely makes comparisons and he loathes expectations, at least publicly. Asked if he knew what he had in that class, he turned the question down. "I don't ever think of it that way," Saban said. "We just try to take the guys from wherever they are and try to develop them so that they can be the best that they can be. And there's some guys that we have very high hopes for and think are going to be great players that don't really pan out, and there's other guys that become great players when you really didn't think that they might become great players.

"So I think we just take each individual player and try to help them develop personally, academically, and athletically so that they can be the best version of themselves and go out and compete and create value for themselves as football players."

The five-star players have largely worked out. Harris, Leatherwood, and Jeudy were as good as advertised. The other two—Dylan Moses and LaBryan Ray—had injuries derail their careers. Moses's severe knee injury that he sustained as a junior bothered him all the way through his senior season in 2020.

Moses's recruitment was eventful. He made headlines as an eighth grader when he earned multiple Power 5 offers. As a

Louisiana native, many assumed he'd go to LSU. But he didn't, and there were some hurt feelings.

At some point, the class started to recruit itself, the momentum and big names becoming a snowball too big to stop. "That was one of the main reasons I committed to Alabama," Moses said. "I wanted to be part of a great team and be surrounded by great competition. That was something that I looked at before I committed. And I knew that us all coming together would be something that would be beneficial later on down the road."

If the class was an unstoppable snowball, what got it started? Look no further than one of the best recruiting staffs Alabama has ever had. Aside from Saban, who's widely considered one of the best ever, others were relentless. To get an accurate picture of the staff, consider the coaches who first started recruiting the athletes and those who wrapped them up. To do that, look at the coaching staffs in 2016 and 2017. They included Jeremy Pruitt, Mario Cristobal, Tosh Lupoi, Mike Locksley, Lane Kiffin, Billy Napier, Derrick Ansley, and Joe Pannunzio. That's a staggering number of quality recruiters, which is why the class ended up the way it did. "I should receive a residual check," one assistant joked.

Defensive lineman Phidarian Mathis looks back and shakes his head. "I'm just proud to say that I'm a part of that," Mathis said.

Harris, who notably hates attention, had a different viewpoint. He didn't really join until he made that decision to get on that plane. He often wonders how things would have been different if he'd gotten on the other one. But it worked out. He started his career with a national championship, and he ended his collegiate career with a national title. It was a nice bookend. "Going back to recruitment, I didn't like it. It's too much attention, way too much attention for me," Harris said. "I think I just showed up here. I just showed up. I didn't even tell them I was coming here. I just showed up. I was tired of it. I popped up at the airport with Tua. And I didn't even know all the recruits that were here.

"So first day of practice, I saw all these recruits I knew in high school. I look around, I'm like, 'Man, we've actually got a pretty good recruiting class here.' I mean, obviously it showed up in the championship game freshman year and now ever since. I think it took off. Coach Saban did a really good job of recruiting. And hopefully we get to bring one home, another natty home."

It was legendary.

PART 4

TRADITIONS

15

"Rammer Jammer"

It comes at you rhythmically at the end of an Alabama victory. Even if you don't know it, you know it. It sounds similar to many a stadium anthem. But "Rammer Jammer" and how it's played, whom it's directed at, and the time at which it's played are uniquely Alabama.

If you don't know the words, they don't take long to learn. Let's say the opponent is Auburn, for example:

Hey, Auburn
Hey, Auburn
Hey, Auburn
We just beat the hell out of you
Rammer Jammer, Yellow Hammer
Give 'em hell, Alabama!

At home or away, as long as the Million Dollar Band is there, and as long as Alabama wins, you can count on "Rammer Jammer" to be played following a Crimson Tide football game.

It's not a complicated piece of music, utilizing just three notes, but it's melodic to the ears of Crimson Tide fans, students, and alumni. It's anything but to fans of other SEC teams who've heard it so much that some have adopted a reverse "Rammer Jammer" to sing back at Alabama. They don't get to sing it much, because let's face it, Alabama doesn't lose often. When you hear "Rammer Jammer," it means one thing: Alabama just beat you, and if it's a Nick Saban–coached Alabama team, it's likely they indeed just beat the hell out of you.

"Rammer Jammer" is not very collegiate. It's in-your-face trash talk coming from the band. It's neither original nor classy. That's what makes it so controversial for academic types and fans of other teams. But students eat it up, as do alumni, and it's a heck of a lot of fun for fans to sing along with the Million Dollar Band on a Saturday night after winning another college football game.

The "Rammer Jammer" cheer existed long before being put into musical form, and the song has seen its share of controversy in its day. When band director Dr. James Ferguson came to Tuscaloosa from Oxford, Mississippi, the cadence to the tune was brought over from Ole Miss in the likeness of "Hotty Toddy." The Alabama version derives its name from the old student magazine titled *Rammer Jammer*. And the yellowhammer is the official state bird. Put them together and you have a sort of rhyming taunt belting from the student section in Bryant-Denny Stadium.

Dr. Kenneth Ozzello, the director of bands at Alabama, came to the university in 1989, and he's overseen the changing of the tradition of "Rammer Jammer" to its current form. "When I first came, it was already sort of a staple, but it was used in a much different way," Ozzello said. "The cheer came with Dr. Ferguson, who was director of the band in the 1980s, and he came to Alabama from Ole Miss. And actually the band called that cheer forever 'the Ole Miss cheer.' It eventually got to be called 'Rammer Jammer.'

"Back then they used to play it all the time. They used to play it before the games. Instead of 'We just,' they'd sing, 'We're going to beat the hell out of you.' They would play it during the games, sometimes several times, [for example] during big moments of the game. But eventually there were some complaints about the cheer because it says 'beat the hell out of you.' And I think maybe in the '90s the band played it like 15 times in a row after beating Tennessee. There was some controversy there. So it's sort of [gotten] pared back. And in fact, there was one year when we weren't allowed to play it at all. But there was such an outcry from the fans that eventually it came back into play, but there were parameters, and the parameters were it had to be a big game and we couldn't play it until the game was in hand. And then eventually we got to the point where we weren't playing it until the clock struck zero."

As Ozzello said, the placement in the game has changed over the years, and probably with good reason. Can you imagine telling Nick Saban that the band was taunting an opponent before the game even began? No thank you. Now it's played only near the end or at the end of a game. Sometimes the cheer gets sung once; sometimes it goes on and on—it depends on the opponent and the significance of the game. After Alabama broke a six-year losing streak to hated in-state rival Auburn in 2008, the Million Dollar Band played it six times. So who makes that call? "I do," Ozzello said. "And I kind of judge it. You know if we're playing East-West-North-South Tech, one will do just fine. If we just won a big SEC game, we almost always play it two times. If it's a really special moment, we'll add a couple more to it."

There is always some discussion too if it the team doesn't soundly defeat an opponent. Should the crowd really be prompted to sing "We just beat the hell out of you" after squeaking by an opponent? Some say to sing it regardless; others think some discretion should be used. Regardless of what side of the issues you fall on, there would be some disappointed people in the stands of Bryant-Denny Stadium if it weren't played.

Some aren't fond of the song at all, asserting that such a taunt shouldn't be featured in a college football game. That line of thinking has been kicked around in the past by UA administrations, but the cheer has survived. If you thought the temporary displacement of "Dixieland Delight" during football games led to a vocal student section, imagine taking away "Rammer Jammer."

It's become something to look forward to so much that some people stick around in a blowout game just to hear the Million Dollar Band play it so they can participate in singing it. The players love it too, often running to the student section in front of the band to celebrate in the singing of it with fellow students. "If people hang around to the end of the game, even if we're winning 60–0, they want to hear it," Ozzello said. "And if somebody has never been to one of those games and their buddy brought them to the game, they say, 'Oh, you've got to wait to the end because it's the best part when we get to sing this cheer.' You know, it's really become a core tradition."

Part of the reason we like college football is its differing traditions across the country. The lack of homogenization is part of the allure. Go to the NFL if you want sameness. "Rammer Jammer" is fun for fans of Alabama and hated by fans of other teams. And that's the way it should be. That's what makes it fun.

16

Bryant-Denny Stadium

"I recognize that this beautiful stadium, of classic design, named in my honor, is the last of almost countless expressions of friendship that have made my life in Alabama happy and contented. I have been honored far beyond anything that I deserve."

—UA President George Hutcheson Denny at the dedication of Denny Stadium on October 5, 1929

I WONDER WHAT GEORGE H. DENNY WOULD SAY IF HE saw his namesake now. It's been more than 90 years since Denny, the University of Alabama's 15th president, oversaw the construction of a permanent on-campus football home. In that time, there have been nine major renovations, the latest reducing capacity to 100,077 in 2020. That renovation, completed during COVID, converted the old press box to new private premium skyboxes for athletic department donors, expanded the seating area, and created more premium seating in all of the eastern portion of the stadium. It came at a cost of $107 million. It also included a tunnel for the team to enter its locker room from outside the stadium and a new recruiting room and larger video boards in the four corners of the stadium.

Prior to that, in 2010, the stadium completed the south end zone addition, which then put capacity at 101,821. There have been a lot of changes to the venue through the years, and especially so since the 1980s.

Bryant-Denny Stadium is one of college football's most impressive venues. The monument to Alabama football, which stands on the nearly nine-acre tract on the southwest side of campus, hardly resembles the modest venue it began as when initially constructed in 1929. Over the years, Bryant-Denny Stadium has undergone several changes—both cosmetic and structural—to evolve from its single-grandstand beginnings to now what many consider one of the finest in all the land. All in all, it's not bad for a building that was for a period considered one of the worst facilities in college football. An estimated $200 million has been pumped into the stadium since the venue was at its lowest point in the mid-1980s. The key under Mal Moore's leadership, and now under Greg Byrne's, is not to stand still.

Originally built in 1929 for $100,000, with monies won from the 1926 and '27 Rose Bowl football teams, what was then called Denny Stadium was a 12,072-seat grandstand on the west side of the field in the likeness of the Yale Bowl, with plans to ultimately expand the stadium to a capacity of 60,000. Seven years later, in 1936, an east grandstand half the size of the west one was constructed. Additions followed in 1946 (with bleachers added to the end zone) and 1951 (making the grandstands the same height to add more seating). When coach Paul W. "Bear" Bryant returned to lead Alabama in 1958, he wanted to construct a new stadium out by Highway 82, where UA's softball complex is now located. When that plan didn't work out, renovations continued on Denny Stadium, and in 1961 a press box and elevator were added. Five years later the university enclosed the end zones, bringing the stadium to its originally planned maximum seating capacity of 60,000.

After 1966 the stadium saw no additions or renovations for 22 years, decaying with each passing year. The stadium was officially renamed Bryant-Denny Stadium in 1976 when late state senator Bert Bank persuaded the Alabama legislature to honor Bryant.

On the field, Alabama football was a national power with very few equals, but its on-campus stadium left a lot to be desired. Tony Pavón has spent years researching Alabama football—in particular Bryant-Denny Stadium—for his website PrideoftheTide.com. By the mid-1980s, he said, the stadium was on its last legs. "The press box got old, the bathrooms were terrible," Pavón said. "The facility itself was 20 years old. Parts of the stadium were 50, 60 years old by then. I remember while I was in high school reading a newspaper article about Bryant-Denny being voted the worst stadium in college football. Heck, up until 1988 the name wasn't even on the stadium anywhere, and then that year they only put it in front of the A-Club entrance."

Former UA player Roger Shultz first saw the stadium as a high school recruit during the 1985 spring game. "It was old and rundown. It surprised me," Shultz said. "I was like, 'This is Alabama?' I was in shock of how bad it was. The restrooms were bad. The locker room was tucked away in the corner of the stadium. It was crazy."

How bad was Bryant-Denny Stadium during the mid-1980s? Consider this excerpt from a front-page story about the floundering venue from a Nov 15, 1986, story in the *Tuscaloosa News*: "Bryant-Denny is really less a stadium than pieces of a stadium stuck together over five decades; a whole that is something less than the sum of its parts suggest. It is a maze of dead ends and occasional byzantine passages; concourses are overburdened at the upper level and underused at the ground level; and it has a system of ramps and gates that makes finding a seat akin to trying to manipulate a colossal combination lock."

Concrete and rebar weren't the only things that needed tending. There were still fiberglass-covered wooden bleachers in the stadium as late as 1993, when UA replaced them with aluminum bleachers and waterproofed the stadium.

The playing surface within the stadium has gotten an upgrade throughout the years as well. The grass in Denny Stadium was hardly kind to players during the 1960s. Jack Rutledge, who was recruited by J. B. "Ears" Whitworth and played for three seasons under Bryant, remembered the field sometimes abusing his body more than the opposition. "The field had spurs on it.... You'd go sliding across the grass and come up with a dozen...stickers in your hand," Rutledge said. "The field was awful. The drainage was bad too. It was a problem."

Astroturf was installed in Denny Stadium for the 1968 season and remained until 1991, when the university went back to grass. The synthetic surface, much like the burr-covered grass field before it, was no picnic on the players. Alabama career tackles leader Wayne Davis said the turf was worn-out by the time he arrived on campus in 1983. "That artificial turf, I tell you, it was hard. It was really hard, there's no doubt about that," he said. "It really wore on your legs and every joint because it didn't give any. And man, the heat that came up from it. You could stand in one end zone and look out and see the heat rising up on it. Its inability to give when you're making a cut and the fact that it heats up a whole lot more, it's a lot more difficult to play on than natural turf. And I've seen some guys, [such as] Cornelius [Bennett], come up with some pretty nasty burns after making a tackle. It wasn't a pretty sight."

Former Alabama facilities director Thad Turnipseed—who had also played on the artificial surface—said there was a reason players wore long sleeves even in warm weather when playing at Bryant-Denny. "It was actually asphalt under the turf, with no padding, and the turf was probably only an inch thick," Turnipseed said. "It felt like falling on concrete. Now, it wasn't as coarse as concrete, but the particles on the turf were bad enough. You'd have rashes all over from the particles on the carpet."

That Alabama played no fewer than three games each season at Birmingham's Legion Field played no small part in Bryant-Denny's neglect. The Magic City was a staple for Alabama football, hosting games since the program's inception in 1892. Alabama played at Lakeview Park, North Birmingham Park, and West End Park from 1905 to 1911, and at the old Alabama State Fairgrounds before moving to Rickwood Field, where they played some games from 1912 to 1927.

Alabama began playing at Legion Field when it was constructed in 1927, and regularly played there until 2003 when the Tide defeated South Florida 40–17 in its last game there. Alabama played all of its home games at Legion Field in 1987, when Bryant-Denny underwent an expansion that added an upper deck on the west side, increasing capacity to 70,123.

When Shultz took the field against Vanderbilt on September 24, 1988—a 44–10 Crimson Tide victory—he was impressed with the addition but immediately wanted more. "I kept looking up at it and wondering, 'When are they going to fill out the other side?'" he said. "It needed some balance." Shultz and the rest of the Alabama fan base would have to wait 10 years for that symmetry to come. The east side got an upper deck for the 1998 season.

Alabama hosted BYU to open that season. Besides the heat, which sent many of his players to the sideline with cramps, LaVell Edwards, the Cougars' Hall of Fame coach, remembers two things about the Tide's 38–31 victory. "We couldn't stop that running back—it felt like he ran for 10 scores," Edwards said of Shaun Alexander's five-touchdown performance. "And it was so loud in there. It just felt like the noise was right on top of you.

"I always preferred playing in venues like that—those great, old, historic stadiums. There's been some great football played there."

If you want to credit one person for getting the lion's share of work and fundraising done, credit a man who spent almost his entire life loving the University of Alabama: Mal Moore. When Moore became Alabama's athletics director in 1999, he soon realized that enhancing athletic facilities and building new ones was job one. He started the athletic department's capital fundraising campaign to raise monies to make new and renovated facilities possible.

What that meant for Bryant-Denny was an upper deck in the north end zone in 2006, which, at the time, Moore thought was the final brushstroke for the historic stadium. But with Moore's hiring of Nick Saban and the subsequent on-the-field success of the Crimson Tide, ticket demands increased and Moore went back to the drawing board.

The 2010 project involved an eight-story expansion, which included 230,000 square feet and an additional 9,000 seats, making Bryant-Denny the fifth-largest on-campus football stadium in the country with official capacity at 101,821. That's decreased now, but the symmetry of the stadium is breathtaking.

"I've gotten in trouble from Coach Moore a couple of times because I've said it's the nicest facility in the country," Turnipseed said in 2010. "So I'll say this: It's as nice as anybody's out there. We're not the biggest, but we're as nice as anybody's."

Moore, who passed in 2013, said expansion was justified from both a supply-and-demand standpoint and to help stay ahead of the curve for recruiting purposes. "Back in my time, I was coming to Alabama because I was just a huge Alabama fan," Moore said in 2010. "But now where things have changed is a recruit can get on his computer and take a virtual tour through the stadium at Palo Alto at Stanford University, and then they can pull yours up and compare, and never leave their bedrooms. It's a different world. Forty years ago that was not the case. That's changed the way you do a lot of things. It's a lot like showing somebody your house. It's yours, it's where you live, and you're proud of it. The way I see Alabama, you know the Crimson Tide is a great name. It has a great tradition. It's powerful. It deserves the best. It has earned that, I think." Turnipseed said the expansion cemented Moore's legacy.

The stadium can now be seen for miles and from several locations across Tuscaloosa. Rising over the UA campus, Bryant-Denny Stadium is now just as identifiable with the University of Alabama as is Denny Chimes or the Quad. "The stadium never really had a presence," Shultz said. "You could be on campus and never really know where the stadium is. Now when you're on campus, you know where the stadium is.

"What I love is not just the stadium. Don't get me wrong, the stadium is beautiful. But it's what it conveys. It's big and powerful. It says, 'By God, we're the best in the country.' That's what the stadium says the most. It says, 'We're No. 1.'"

That stadium has continued to take shape in the 12 years since the 2010 renovation, and it's been a whirlwind of activity that has involved more than just seating capacity. Current leaders have to worry about keeping fans coming to the games and not content to stay at home and watch games from their couches and recliners. And part of that is the fostering of a more pleasant in-stadium experience, which includes better concession choices, bathrooms, and cell phone reception and Wi-Fi on campus and in the stadium during game days. And those things continue to evolve. Just like running a college football team, the job is never finished. You must anticipate what the needs will be. That's part of the job of athletic director Greg Byrne. "Well, right now we know we have concession issues," Byrne said in the fall of 2021. And sometimes there's human error involved, but there's also issues where what's wrong with the concession stands is that they're 60 to 70 years old. These concession stands were built for a stadium with 30,000 to 40,000 people in them. Bryant-Denny came up out of the ground and evolved to where it is today. There were improvements that we made to the overall concession experience. But there [are] a lot of them that haven't been touched in years. And so when people get frustrated that we logistically can't get a hot dog to them, I don't blame them, right?"

Fans have every game played available on their televisions, and they don't have to go to campus to watch. That's something previous generations of team leaders didn't really have to concern themselves with. So easy, affordable concessions are a part of the conversation. As is comfortable seating. As is bringing in good opponents. Everything must be considered, even upgrading and improving things that fans don't see—things such as new elevators, wiring, maintenance, and upkeep of the existing structure and infrastructure. Those come with big price tags, and no one outside of those responsible for the work sees those things being done.

But the fan experience is the No. 1 thing when it comes to stadium enhancement. Competing with television is a real concern and is the elephant in the room with every decision that's made in regard to Bryant-Denny Stadium renovations. "We talk about it all the time," Byrne said. "Why did we change our nonconference schedule approach? We wanted to create value for season ticket holders to where they say, 'Man, I can come in and be here for an Alabama–Ohio State game down the road and Alabama–Notre Dame game and Alabama-Texas and Alabama-Oklahoma.' That gets people excited, that keeps them engaged, because if you don't engage them, they'll go find something else. And I am part of what we do with the stadium lights and, you know, the music. The atmosphere we're trying to create is something to get them to say, 'I can't get that at home.' Right? So it's worth it to them to have to come early to walk distances to get to the stadium to get to their seats. This is just a different experience."

The LED lights have definitely upgraded the in-stadium experience. It's especially an experience for night games. One of the indelible images of the 2021 season was Nick Saban kneeling and talking to quarterback Bryce Young on the sideline and the crimson LED lights creating a background that stood out. That was a substantial cost to the athletic department. Fans' feedback has proved the cost worth it. "The old lights were past their usefulness," Byrne said. "And if you watch some of the games from the past, there was a yellow tint starting to be seen. And so as we were exploring what LED lights we wanted to use. We were informed that they were now able to start doing some LED lights with color capabilities, where you didn't have to turn the lights off and turn the other ones on. And it could be simultaneous. And so when we did that, or we started looking at it, the price really wasn't much different, and we decided, 'Hey, might as well' since we were starting this, and we were able to work with Musco Lighting and put this together."

The lights can now be synced with music that plays in the stadium to create light shows. It seems silly and has absolutely nothing to do with football, but the new LED lights 100 percent create more of an atmosphere that fans can enjoy.

It's just one thing that UA leadership anticipated and planned for in this new age of competing for fans. Expect that to continue as that battle rages on. Bryant-Denny Stadium gives them a large canvas on which to experiment, and there's more to come in the next planned renovation.

17
How Many Titles?

WANT TO DIVIDE THE ALABAMA FAN BASE REAL QUICK? ASK a question about how many football national championships the program has won, and you'll get a confident statement from some and a shifty-eyed, less confident answer from others. Whether you claim 18 national titles, as the University of Alabama officially does, or whether you count only AP titles, the confusion is to be expected. It's not Alabama's fault. It's college football's fault.

There is no official overseer of college football, and as dumb as that sounds, it's frustratingly the truth. The NCAA doesn't regulate an official championship like it does for other collegiate sports. It does for basketball, and that sport's champion is decided by the NCAA Tournament. But football is under the umbrella of no such authority—only a group of presidents and commissioners, all with their own beliefs and agendas. If there were one body overseeing the sport, these things wouldn't happen.

THE PROGRAM: ALABAMA

But college football's been like that throughout its history. The playoff is only a recent departure from the way the sport determined its champion throughout the majority of its history. Before that, of course, was the BCS, where computers set the stage for the top two teams to play for a title. Before even that, though, it was determined by voters. Media members and others who would watch games and then, through their own methodologies, would place a ranking beside each team. At the end of the season, they would assign a final ranking next to each team, and whoever had the most points ended up No. 1. And much like today, each team's schedule was different, with varying degrees of difficulty. But at least today, there's an apparatus at the end of the season to place the four highest-ranked teams and have them play it off. Prior to that, the final vote was it: "Here's your champion."

All of this informs why there is no "official" list for how many national titles have been won by an individual school. It has sort of been left to each institution to make their own determination of how many titles to claim. You can see the problem here. Which is why Alabama claims 18 national championships and other programs and fans around the country scoff.

How did Alabama arrive at that number? Here's the story. No one can argue that Alabama has six national titles in the Nick Saban era. Other fans, hate it as they might, can't deny that. He won them all during the BCS or CFP era. Those championships happened on the field. Alabama beat Texas to win the 2009 title. It beat LSU to win the 2011 title. It beat Notre Dame to win in 2012. It defeated Clemson to win the 2015 championship, Georgia for 2017, and Ohio State for 2020. The math on that, angry as it might make the detractors of Crimson Tide football, can't be debated. But beyond that? Buckle up.

So how many football national championships has Alabama won? Now that's a straightforward but oh-so-tricky question. With the success the Crimson Tide has enjoyed under Nick Saban, that total has changed seemingly every other year or so, but the question is worthy of exploration because the answer it reveals is one of pride, controversy, derision, and great misunderstanding. It also has more than one answer, depending on which selectors you subscribe to and when you begin recognizing championships.

For the record, Alabama claims 18 national titles. That leads to one of two arguments: It's more than it should claim, say critics. It's less than it could claim, according to the NCAA's FBS record book, in which listed historical selectors credit UA with as many as 22 possible titles.

There's nothing in between. When this topic is tackled, the college football public falls on one side or the other. But there is no "right" answer because college football stands alone in its quirkiness of how it determines its champion. There's a certain charm and character to that, to be sure, that makes the sport unlike its professional counterpart. Critics will argue the opposite and say that it's a flaw and there's nothing charming about it whatsoever. Nevertheless, from the beginning of the Associated Press poll in 1936 through the end of the BCS era in 2013, the champion was determined not on the field but at least partially by voters. And that's not even taking into account the myriad champions chosen by different people, organizations, and formulas, some retroactive to the sport's beginning in 1869.

Alabama certainly doesn't stand alone in the weirdness of how many national championships it says it has won. Other schools have retroactively added championships, as has Alabama. We'll get to that later. But Alabama has won so many titles, and there is debate surrounding the legitimacy of some of those claims. Simply put, Alabama stands out from the rest because it has so many unbeaten national championships that critics say, "Why add to the tally with dubious claims?" The AP poll has crowned a national champion since 1936. During that time, the Crimson Tide has laid claim to 12 (1961, 1964, 1965, 1978, 1979, 1992, 2009, 2011, 2012, 2015, 2017, and 2020) AP titles, the most of any program in the nation. The next-closest? Notre Dame, with eight. So even if you take away all the debated and disputed national championships that Alabama boasts, it still has the most by a healthy margin.

That makes it exasperating for critics, some of whom take issue with national championships claimed before the AP poll began in 1936. Alabama claims four national titles before 1936 (1925, 1926, 1930, and 1934). Then there remains 1941. Perhaps no championship in the history of sports is more debated than Alabama claiming 1941. No, 1941 is a conversation unto itself, but we'll get to that later.

Here's where things get interesting. Alabama didn't always claim all these championships. The story of how it came to is one of the more fascinating quirks in Crimson Tide history. There was no intent to brag or boast, only to recognize. Up until 1984, Alabama proudly recognized six national championship teams, all under the leadership of legendary coach Paul W. "Bear" Bryant. Those title squads are 1961, 1964, 1965, 1973, 1978, and 1979. Five of those are championships awarded by the AP, and one—1973—is a recognized UPI coaches' poll title, in the last season either of the two polls crowned its champion before the bowls.

So how did the university go from only recognizing six titles to the pre–poll era titles? A summer research project, that's how. On the last page of the 1983 media guide, Alabama listed Bryant's six national championships. That season was the first after Bryant's retirement and subsequent death. Former All-American split end Ray Perkins assumed the head coaching duties, and one of his first hires was Wayne Atcheson, also a UA graduate, whom he installed as sports information director. Atcheson was a student worker under Bryant when the coach really had things humming in the 1960s, and he had compiled press clippings of those great teams from 1964, 1965, and 1966 into scrapbooks. He spent literally hours constructing those. To do so, he immersed himself in Alabama football history. It was a project he threw himself into and one he loved.

Atcheson was enthralled with the rich tradition, the great teams of the past. So when he got the SID job, one of the first things he did was dig around and find those scrapbooks in the bowels of what was then named Memorial Coliseum (now Coleman Coliseum). Then he got to thinking. He thought it was a shame that some of those teams from the pre-Bryant era weren't properly memorialized. It grated on him that the media guide and official football stationery recognized titles only from teams coached by Bryant. Not even Bryant's undefeated 1934 team—which won the Rose Bowl and on which Atcheson had played end opposite legendary receiver Don Hutson—was celebrated. He thought the university's official records should reflect the full history of the program and that those great teams should be honored.

Atcheson had never thought that the official Alabama football records, which listed only six national championships, told the whole story. He dug into the record books and came up with five additional Alabama teams that he thought deserved to be recognized by the school as national champions. When he put together the 1984 media guide, the last page featured 11 national championships. In the pages directly before that, he detailed every national championship–winning team in program history, adding 1925, 1926, 1930, 1934, and 1941. Overnight, Alabama went from 6 national titles to 11.

Hardly anyone noticed. There was no promotional material printed. There's wasn't a public relations blitz to get the word out. Nothing happened. It wasn't meant to be what it has become. Football went on in Tuscaloosa, and not a soul gave much attention to Alabama claiming five more national championships. It served the sole purpose of internally recognizing great teams of the past.

That is, until 1992. That's when it shifted, and Atcheson could never have guessed how it would take off. When the Crimson Tide went 13–0 in 1992 and added another national championship trophy to the case, the marketing of 12 national championships became a sort of cottage industry in the state. It had been 13 years since the last national title, and while that's not a long time for most programs, after the success and title runs under Bryant in the 1960s and 1970s, it felt like an eternity. So anything that could be licensed with Alabama football and 12 national championships printed on it was produced. I'm talking T-shirts, bumper stickers, and other memorabilia of all sorts that now hailed Alabama as the home of 12 national championship teams. There were even watches made with each hour represented by a different national championship team. Radio talk shows picked up on it. Rival fans seized upon it. The debate was on.

Truth be told, Atcheson never intended it to be anything of the sort. Decades later, he said he was surprised when people took issue with it. "I'm still shocked that I was even asked about it," Atcheson said. "People say, 'Mr. Atcheson, it seems like you're the guy that claimed five championships.' Because I never thought about it in a comparative way. I felt like it was just something that needed to be done or had not been done. It was something that should be added, you know, the fact that we had those teams that hadn't been recognized correctly."

In today's landscape, where the CFP has essentially made bowl games an afterthought, it's hard to envision championships not being the focus. But believe it or not, there was a time in the not-so-distant past when national championships just weren't that big of a deal. That's not saying they weren't important or that they weren't valued. But they weren't the be-all and end-all that they seem to be in this age when ESPN discusses and debates the CFP nearly all season long, dedicating hours and hours of programming to tracking teams and their pursuits of a title.

You want proof that things were different once upon a time? Look no further than how Bryant informed his 1965 Alabama team that it had won the title, vaulting from No. 4 in the AP poll after it beat No. 3 Nebraska in the Orange Bowl, and No. 1 Michigan State and No. 2 Arkansas lost. It was the first time the AP had crowned its champion after the bowls. He didn't call a team meeting. There was no announcement on television. "Coach Bryant wrote them a note," Atcheson said. "He gets the word at four in the morning that the 1965 team won the national championship from the AP after the bowl game. Someone called him up and said, 'Congratulations, Coach, you're the national champion.' That's how he found out. Then he writes a note. We're in Paul Bryant Hall, and he just puts the note at the desk where the guys check in at the lobby. It was something like, 'Congratulations, men. You've just won, and now you're the national champion.'"

One can easily envision a championship during that time before the BCS and CFP being viewed as similar to a mythical high school national championship today, where the top teams don't play each other. When teams don't play each other, a voted national championship just doesn't have the same feeling attached. That's how differently time has treated the importance of national championships. And that's sort of where Atcheson's intentions intersected with the reality of how disingenuous some of Alabama's title claims are currently viewed to be. The proud Alabama alumnus never intended for those championships to be recognized with T-shirts and plaques on the Walk of Champions. Not that he's against it, but that was never his goal. He simply didn't want those teams and their respective accomplishments to be overshadowed by the university recognizing only Bryant's six titles. To him, it was more about internal recognition than external.

"I didn't even think about the other schools," Atcheson said. "At that time, we all knew Notre Dame had more than anybody. And you know, Notre Dame—it wasn't about having more than them. In recruiting, they got the cream of the crop. They could recruit the whole nation. And we just accepted Notre Dame as the kingpin of college football. But Alabama had great tradition that really made football in the South what it was. Alabama was the team in the South that paved the way for everybody else. And we weren't even recognizing those teams in the 1920s or 1930s, not even Coach Bryant's team in '34. It was just purely a school thing to recognize those past teams, and not a thought was given whatsoever to [championships] anybody else had."

Given that context, what should be made of Alabama's 18 national championships? Even the most fervent Alabama hater can't take any issue with the Crimson Tide's 12 AP national titles. College football historians disagree about what to make of the Rose Bowl winners. Alabama's famous 20–19 win against Washington in the 1926 Rose Bowl is arguably the most important game ever played in relation to Southern football. It's called the Game that Changed the South for how it put college football in the South on the map. That game produced UA's first national championship (1925). However, two other teams are listed as recognized national champions that year too (Dartmouth, which claims a title, and Michigan, which doesn't).

Arizona Daily Star columnist Billy Evans captured the national landscape when the dust settled on the season. Just like today, there was regional disagreement. "The best football team in the country? I beg to pass on that one," Evans wrote. "The best football team is largely a matter of where you happen to reside. It's a question to start an argument. For the first time in years, the sectional supremacy in football is well defined. Only in the South is there a real dispute. The East is overwhelmingly for Dartmouth, while the West favors Michigan. Washington holds the coast honors, while Alabama and Tulane are the choice of the South. Alabama was voted the Pickens trophy by a committee of southern newspaper men. That award is equivalent to being named the champion." That was the first of Alabama's national championships and the origin of the line in "Yea Alabama"—the fight song—that goes, "Remember the Rose Bowl, we'll win then."

But not everyone agrees those titles should be counted. "I tend to view any national championship awarded before the AP poll began in 1936 with a raised eyebrow," college football historian and acclaimed writer Ivan Maisel said. "And I was chastised about that by Dan Jenkins, who defended Dickinson and then Dunkel as rating systems. And there were a couple other people who were giving out championships before the AP. I didn't know who had credibility before 1936. College football was always a regional sport; nobody cared about the national championship. And it wasn't really contested until, in my mind, the AP started handing them out.

"So that's the one thing I think of, and the other is that just, in general, there's always been sort of a laissez-faire attitude toward claiming a national championship, at least before the BCS. And if you wanted to claim it, and you wanted to buy the rings and sell the T-shirts, nobody really objected all that much, which, again, spoke to the regional nature of the sport."

Only one national championship calls into question the entire lot of Crimson Tide titles, though. That's the 1941 crown awarded by Houlgate. The Houlgate system was an analytical ranking of teams created by Deke Houlgate, whose rankings ran from 1927 to 1958 and were published in newspapers and magazines. Alabama finished the 1941 season 9–2 with losses to Mississippi State and Vanderbilt. Alabama beat some quality teams, but with two conference losses and no SEC title—not to mention a final AP ranking of No. 20 before the Cotton Bowl— it's a large leap to expect others to recognize that team as a champion.

Keith Dunnavant, an author who has chronicled Bryant, Alabama's 1966 team, and Bart Starr, among other topics, sums up the general feeling of how claiming 1941 casts aspersions on some of the other titles. Houlgate is a recognized selection in the NCAA's FBS record book, which has ceded that territory to too many bodies to be taken seriously. "I've never recognized 1941," Dunnavant said. "Unfortunately, Alabama's decision to claim that title has enabled people who don't understand how the system worked in the pre–wire service era to snipe at the 1925, '26, '30, and '34 championships, which are legitimate."

Alabama fans have always answered those criticisms by throwing the unbeaten 1966 team into the equation. That team was defending back-to-back national championships and went undefeated that season but was somehow snubbed and finished third in the AP poll. Can you imagine a team now winning two consecutive championships and going undefeated and being denied a title? It was even the subject of Dunnavant's book *The Missing Ring*, although he is crystal-clear that he doesn't think UA should claim that title either.

When choosing teams to remember as champions in 1984, Atcheson said the 1966 team finished third, so there was nothing to consider, although the NCAA record book shows UA has been awarded the designation by Berryman and Sagarin (Elo-Chess). "We were still so close to '66," Atcheson said. "Because everybody knew what happened there. I mean, it'd be hard to put '66 down there. Because we ended up third. I didn't have a lot of access to records, like you're talking about [with the NCAA record book]. And besides, in that day, you know, people weren't boasting about who had the most championships. It was just solely a one-school decision. I wasn't trying to outdo anybody, but it just seems to me that I thought those teams had been recognized as national champions. You know, back in those early days, those selections were what they had to go by."

Should the NCAA be more selective regarding which organizations it lists in its record book? Of course. But what's done is done. And what's the NCAA to do with championships awarded before 1936? It's really just a free-for-all in terms of what universities choose to claim. The NCAA, which does not officially crown a national champion at the FBS level, lists more than 40 different organizations that have awarded national championships. It's pure chaos. Which goes back to the original thought that college football isn't overseen by any one body that could serve as an official record holder for championships. And it's worse for it.

Which puts the onus on Alabama. It's clear what Atcheson intended grew beyond that. He sought to honor players, coaches, and teams that had accomplished great things. Those teams hadn't been given the same recognition as others within the athletic department. He intended to correct it. Marketing, being what it is, though, took things in a different direction. Should Alabama still claim 1941? It looks foolish to do so, but it's probably too late to unring that bell now.

"I think it makes them look silly," Maisel said. "We can all read, and we all know what happened. So why do it, right? What do you gain, and especially at Alabama, what do you gain? It's clear in my mind that they've lost more than they've gained from doing it. I mean, is anybody really gonna recoil because Alabama's only won 16 national championships instead of 18? Right? I don't think so.

"But who in the Mal Moore Building is going to come out and say, 'Yeah, we really need to give that one back.' I would love for Greg [Byrne] to do that. But it's not gonna happen, right?"

At the end of the day, Alabama still has bragging rights. No matter which criteria you use, how many you count, it still has more national championships than any other program. "And that's what's crazy about it," Maisel said. "The last program that needs to claim national championships is Alabama."

18

The Tide Don't Lose in Baton Rouge

ONE OF THE MORE UNUSUAL FACTS IN A SPORT KNOWN FOR the unusual exists between SEC West rivals Alabama and LSU. It's not a surprise that historically Alabama has dominated the series between the two, because Alabama dominates the series history with almost any program it plays on a regular basis. The uniqueness, though, comes in how Alabama has held LSU in a vise grip in games played in Baton Rouge. In those games, the Crimson Tide is an overwhelming 29–9–2 against LSU, including 16–1–1 from 1965 to 1998.

In the Nick Saban era, Alabama has lost in Baton Rouge only once, compiling a road record of 6–1.

2008: Alabama 27–21 (OT)

2010: LSU 24–21

2012: Alabama 21–17

2014: Alabama 20–13 (OT)
2016: Alabama 10–0
2018: Alabama 29–0
2020: Alabama 55–17

For much of the Saban era, the game between the Crimson Tide and the LSU Tigers was must-see TV. Many years it played a direct role in which team had a direct path to the national championship or playoff. Nearly every year it had a say in which team won the SEC West. A lot of years it was so anticipated that it was broadcast during prime time. It's been the most physical game in the SEC in the Saban era. The overall record of the series during this time is 12–4, including the 21–0 win in New Orleans for the national championship. Two of those four losses came during seasons in which the Tigers won a national championship (2007 and 2019).

So what led to the dominance against a team that's had just as much success as any program not named Alabama during that time? There have been close games, including three overtime games. Alabama pulled away most times. In LSU's four wins, the average margin of victory was 4.5 points. In Alabama's 12 wins, the average margin of victory was 14.9 points.

But the focus here is on how Alabama has absolutely owned the Tigers in their home stadium. Here's a closer look at Alabama at LSU in the Saban era. Remember the old saying, "The Tide don't lose in Baton Rouge."

2008

It was arguably the most intense of these games because it was Saban's first game back in Baton Rouge after returning to college football. He'd left LSU to become the Miami Dolphins' head coach after the 2004 season. He spent two seasons in

Miami, and when he went back to college football and chose one of LSU's rivals to do so, the hatred began and the rivalry reached unseen heights.

Alabama had the better team, ranked No. 1 in the country and 9–0 against an LSU team coming off a national championship at No. 15 and 6–2. The Tigers had already lost to Florida and Georgia. Alabama had played a few close games to that point too, including a three-point home win over Kentucky and a four-point home win over Ole Miss. So this game and the way it played out wasn't terribly surprising.

Alabama marched down the field on its first drive and looked poised to take a touchdown lead when disaster struck. John Parker Wilson hit Earl Alexander for a 25-yard gain, but as Alexander was stretching the ball out to score, LSU safety Chad Jones knocked the ball out of his hands for a touchback.

The teams traded touchdowns, and LSU then had a seven-point lead with the ball late in the first half. Jarrett Lee's pass was intercepted by UA safety Rashad Johnson, who returned it 54 yards for the game-tying touchdown.

In the second half, the teams traded touchdowns to tie the game at 21. Alabama had a chance to win it at the end of regulation but Leigh Tiffin's 29-yard field goal was blocked, sending the game into overtime.

Johnson got his second interception of the game in the first overtime period, and on its first play of overtime, Alabama went for the jugular. Wilson hit freshman wide receiver Julio Jones down the left sideline for a 23-yard gain down to the 2. After a Glen Coffee one-yard run, Wilson snuck it in for the 27–21 win.

Saban had downplayed the emotion, but he acknowledged afterward that it was a tough week. "We have special memories of this place," he said. "We always will, and no one will ever tarnish those no matter what they do.

"It's really not sweeter clinching the [SEC] West in Tiger Stadium," Saban said, his voice rising. "It really isn't. My emotions for this place are positive, not negative. I didn't leave LSU to go to Alabama. I left LSU to go to Miami. Myself and my family learned that we didn't like professional football as much as we liked college. So we had the best opportunity to return to college football at the University of Alabama. There is nothing personal in that for me."

As Saban mentioned, the win captured the SEC West division crown for the Crimson Tide, the first time it had done so since 1999. But No. 1 Alabama had different goals, and this game showed them how tough achieving them would be. "We are at about 19,000 feet," Saban said. "The mountain is at 26,000 feet, and the air is changing a little bit. The air is a little rarer."

2010

The lone loss in Baton Rouge of the Saban era might be best remembered for what Les Miles did during the game. The CBS camera crew caught Miles during a timeout reaching down and plucking a blade of grass from the field, plopping it in his mouth, and eating it. It was the game Miles ate grass, and it was the only game he won at home against Alabama with Saban as the head coach.

Alabama entered as the No. 5 team at 7–1 with No. 12 LSU also at 7–1. Alabama had lost to South Carolina and LSU to Auburn. It was a back-and-forth game into the fourth quarter when, with LSU trailing by one and facing fourth-and-1 on the Alabama 26, Miles dialed up the tricks he was known for during his career. He ran a reverse to tight end DeAngelo Peterson, who ran for 23 yards to the UA 3. LSU scored three plays later, and the Tigers held on for the eventual 24–21 win.

For Saban it was another example he could use to illustrate to his team how worrying about outcomes and focusing on the wrong things leads to results like that. The 2010 team is always used as that example. The team was talented and flush with first-round NFL Draft selections, but coming off a championship the year before, that team didn't prepare the way it had the year before. They paid the price for that too.

"This whole year, everyone around us has been very concerned about the results in comparison to what was accomplished a year ago, and that has not been the best thing for the development of this team," Saban said. "They have become too results-oriented, and we never have developed to become as good a team as we can be. How we respond to this will show us what kind of character we have and what kind of pride we have."

The team went on to lose another game, the Iron Bowl, in which it led by three touchdowns before losing. It was just another example of scoreboard watching instead of staying in the moment and doing the job from play to play.

Funny enough, all these years later, the game is still remembered for what Miles did in a moment of stress. He was always viewed as a man unafraid to throw caution to the wind when the game was on the line. He had gone for multiple fourth downs during the game. He had pulled out creative fake field goals. In this game, he chewed on some grass. "I have a little tradition that humbles me as a man, that lets me know that I'm a part of the field and part of the game," Miles said. "You should have seen some games before this. I can tell you one thing: The grass in Tiger Stadium tastes best."

2012

In all my years of covering Alabama games, this is the most memorable Alabama-LSU game. It wasn't the most well-played game. It wasn't even the most dramatic game, given this series has produced multiple overtime games. But it's the one that stands out most to me.

Who knows why games stick with some more than others? Sports are funny that way. They all connect to us in different ways. This one stuck out to me because I covered the game from the stands, in the upper deck where they put the Alabama fans. I wasn't in the press box for this one. I wanted to cover a game and really feel it, not a sanitized version of it in the no-cheering press box. I felt the rise and fall of Alabama fans as the Tide controlling the first half morphed into the offense doing absolutely nothing in the second half. Then suddenly Alabama had the ball trailing by three points on its own 28-yard line with just 1:27 remaining in the game. The game seemed lost, and the fans around me were pretty subdued.

The Alabama offense had all but disappeared in the second half. Quarterback AJ McCarron was 1-for-7 in the second half before that final drive. Death Valley was rocking. It really did seem like a lost cause. And then it happened.

McCarron got into a rhythm with wide receiver Kevin Norwood, and before I knew it Alabama was in LSU territory. McCarron had connected on back-to-back-to-back passes to Norwood covering 18, 15, and 11 yards, respectively. The Tide had the ball on the LSU 28 and had only used 27 seconds. After an incompletion to Norwood in the end zone, McCarron dropped back and T. J. Yeldon let a rushing defender go right by him, and he made himself open for a screen pass. Yeldon caught it and raced 28 yards for the game-winning touchdown.

It was a blur. The team that had done nothing the entire second half had gone down the field lightning-quick for a score. LSU had played soft in the secondary, off the receivers, and Norwood made them pay. It was a dramatic win, and it broke LSU hearts. On the way back to my car, I heard multiple LSU fans seemingly accept their fate as long as Saban was at Alabama. Of course, that wasn't totally true. LSU won the 2019 national championship, although it did so with a new coach (Ed Orgeron). But the point remains, as LSU hasn't beat Alabama at home since.

The emotion came pouring out of McCarron after that touchdown. He went to the bench after that play, hung his head, and cried tears of joy. "There's just so many emotions running through me," McCarron said. "Sometimes it can be a lot of pressure playing here at this university, especially with all the tradition of winning and everything. Just coming back and winning a game like that, and like Coach Saban said, it might be known as the Drive for the history of Alabama. And just to be a part of it with my teammates was just truly a blessing."

2014

Oh, you thought you were done with Alabama-LSU dramatics? Not so fast, my friend! This one involved a late fumble, a last-minute drive, a field goal to get it into overtime, and a trick play in overtime. And Lane Kiffin showed his brilliance as Alabama somehow snatched another victory from the grasp of a crushed LSU team.

It wasn't an offensive game, as defenses ruled the day. Alabama had 315 total yards; LSU had 259. There were exactly three touchdowns scored in the game, and two of those came in regulation.

Just like it had in 2012, it certainly looked like the game could be over for Alabama. With the score tied at 10 with 1:50 remaining, Alabama had the ball at its own 1. T. J. Yeldon gave the offense a bit of space with a five-yard run on first down, but on the very next play, he fumbled and LSU recovered. Game over. Or so everyone thought. The defense stood tall and forced a field goal. Then a critical error by LSU gave Alabama hope. Trent Domingue booted the kickoff out of bounds, and Alabama started at the 35 without having to use any clock. With 50 seconds remaining, quarterback Blake Sims had time to get the team into field goal range to extend the game into overtime, and that's exactly what he did.

On the first play of overtime, Alabama reached into its bag of tricks and called a play where it got an offensive lineman eligible by formation and Brandon Greene caught a Sims past right up the hash down to the 1-yard line. A personal foul penalty moved the ball back, but Alabama had all the momentum. A few plays later, Kiffin got a defensive look he liked, and he changed the play to get an open DeAndrew White into the end zone for a touchdown. "When the ball was in the air, my heart stopped beating," Blake Sims said.

The defense held, and Alabama had somehow won another game in Death Valley it had no business winning.

That's how Alabama has the record it does against LSU in Baton Rouge. Faced with long odds once and again, the Crimson Tide managed to find ways to win the games. Call it a clutch gene or blame it on mistakes made by the other team. Whatever you care to attribute it to, Alabama takes advantage of opportunities and makes LSU pay.

This is the last game played in Baton Rouge that had as much drama. The 2016 matchup was close, as you'll see, but it didn't provide the my-heart-is-in-my-throat moments that 2012 and 2014—and 2008 too, for that matter—did.

2016

It was another low-scoring affair in Death Valley. Par for the course in this series, with the defenses leading the way. In the fourth quarter Alabama continued to shut out the Tigers and got just enough points to remain unbeaten.

The Alabama defense was loaded this season, and LSU managed a paltry six first downs and 125 yards. It was the first of two shutouts in a row in this series in Baton Rouge.

Offensively, it showed how Alabama's offense was changing. It was explosive play after explosive play, but having a dual-threat quarterback made all the difference in this one. Freshman quarterback Jalen Hurts scored the game's only touchdown when he scrambled for a score in the fourth quarter.

After the game, I asked Nick Saban if his team would have won that game without Hurts, a quarterback who could run. He was noncommittal, but the answer was fairly obvious. "I don't know," Saban said. "We made some errors early in the game that were costly, and we got some plays in the end that his athleticism allowed him to make. I think as we grow with him, we're going to have to live with both. I like the second part better than the first."

It was a 21-yard touchdown run on a scramble on a called sprint-out pass to the right. But Hurts kept it all the way and outraced the Tigers defenders to the end zone. The scramble put the bow on a 12-play, 90-yard, 5:57 drive. "He just saw a lane and went for it," left guard Ross Pierschbacher said. "He's able to make those plays because he's so athletic. That adds a huge dimension to our offense. I think he's a spark plug."

It's also kind of comical to think of the quarterback numbers considering what we saw three years later in the battle between Tua Tagovailoa and Joe Burrow. Hurts and LSU quarterback Danny Etling combined to throw for 199 yards and two interceptions with no touchdowns. In 2019, Tagovailoa and Hurts combined to throw for 811 yards, 7 touchdowns, and 1 interception.

But this game was all about defense. The Crimson Tide got five sacks. Saban found a creative adjective to describe his defense: *hateful.* "You can talk about winning ugly, and maybe it wasn't always pretty, because we certainly didn't execute and do things the way we'd like, but you've got to give LSU a lot of credit," Saban said. "It was a tough atmosphere for us out there, but our defense was outstanding. We've got some pretty hateful guys that play defense around here that are pretty good competitors. When they get challenged a little bit, they usually respond, and I think they responded really well tonight."

How stifling was the Crimson Tide defense? LSU didn't run a single play inside the Alabama 30.

2018

It's funny going back and studying these games, how many of them become known for one particular play, player, or strange event. In 2010 it was Les Miles eating grass. In 2012 it was AJ McCarron hitting T. J. Yeldon. In 2014 it was the Brandon Greene trick play. In 2018 it wasn't even the play on the field that was the most memorable. It was a redheaded LSU student staring and not breaking eye contact with the CBS cameras while Alabama was handily winning the game.

No one came blame her because her team was shut out for the second straight time at home by Alabama as the Crimson Tide won 29–0. This is also known as the Quinnen Williams game. The star defensive lineman couldn't be blocked as Alabama owned the line of scrimmage against the Joe Burrow–led offense. Burrow only threw for 184 yards and an interception in the shutout. Williams was overpowering with 10 tackles, 3.5 tackles for loss, and 2.5 sacks.

It was a highly touted game too, matching No. 1 Alabama (8–0) against No. 4 LSU (7–1). But it was clear throughout the game that the Tigers couldn't match up with Alabama in the trenches on either side of the ball. "Alabama overpowered us," LSU coach Ed Orgeron said. "When you max-protect and you're doing everything you can with protection and they're beating you, you've got to look at personnel. You've got to get better. I don't think it was scheme at all. There was nothing we could do about it."

Quarterback Tua Tagovailoa had a good game with 295 yards passing, two touchdown passes, and a memorable scramble for a touchdown. Tagovailoa was hobbled a bit on the 44-yard run that put the game away. "I'd seen the opening, I ran. I was just trying to get the first down," Tagovailoa said. "Once I passed the 30, though, I felt my leg [hurting], and I was going off momentum after that."

The win was Alabama's eighth straight over LSU, and the Tigers faithful were getting restless. That streak would end the next year in a 46–41 shootout in Tuscaloosa that was attended by former President Trump. These two teams have hooked up for some classics in the Saban era, and that was certainly one of them.

Before the 2018 game, the Alabama team was suffering slings and arrows of college football analysts who weren't that impressed with the team's schedule to that point. The team took note of that talk and felt they something to prove. "We really wanted to make a statement in this game," Saban said. "A lot of people talk about our schedule. What better opportunity is there to make a statement than the circumstance we were in?"

2020

LSU had just won the game the year before, breaking Alabama's eight-game winning streak. That's enough to want revenge, but there were other things too. There was the way LSU players had gone to the section of Bryant-Denny Stadium to try to convince recruits attending the game to choose LSU instead. There was an LSU player broadcasting the postgame locker room celebration live, during which Ed Orgeron said the following: "We're going to beat their ass in recruiting! We're going to beat their ass every time they see us! You understand me? Roll Tide, what? Fuck you!"

Now stuff like that is usually fan fodder, things that fan bases discuss the week of the game to hype it up. Players hear it too, no doubt, but once the game starts, past words spoken have literally no impact on the winner and loser of the contest. But they did serve as motivation in the days leading up to the game. Words can't help you win a game, but they can help you prepare to win one.

Alabama got its revenge on the field, blowing out the Tigers by 38 points, one of the largest margins of victory in series history. LSU had no answers. Mac Jones and DeVonta Smith did. Jones threw for 385 yards and 4 touchdowns, 3 of them to Smith, who had 231 yards receiving. One touchdown catch stands out. Smith jumped up and snagged a one-handed touchdown grab in the back of the end zone. It was all the more fitting for Smith, who hails from Amite, Louisiana.

It was after Smith's performance and that highlight catch when college football as a whole began thinking that a wide receiver could win the Heisman Trophy. A receiver hadn't done so since Desmond Howard did it in 1991. But Smith grabbed everyone's attention that night. "He's probably done as much this year for our team as any player that we've ever had," Saban said. "He's a great leader on the team. It's not fair to compare him to somebody else that you didn't even see, but I don't think there's many players in the country that have done more for their team than Smitty does for our team."

Running back Najee Harris had a field day too, rushing for 145 yards and 3 touchdowns. It was a tail whipping rarely seen in this series. It was also one of the signs that things weren't heading in the right direction for Orgeron, who the season before had won a national championship. But for Alabama, LSU was just another speed bump on the path to a national championship. The 2020 Alabama team was one of the greatest in college football history.

Four Alabama assistant coaches missed the game due to being quarantined. Sal Sunseri, Karl Scott, Freddie Roach, and Holmon Wiggins were all in Tuscaloosa as the coaching staff had to make some adjustments. That's 40 percent of the on-the-field assistant coaching staff.

Saban highlighted the fact that his players didn't overly celebrate the win, and it was a noted difference in the discipline of both programs. The Alabama players hadn't forgotten what the LSU players did on their field the year before, but the Crimson Tide was playing for something bigger.

PART 5

19

Aaron Douglas

AARON DOUGLAS WASN'T AROUND TO EXPERIENCE THE thrill of winning a national championship. But he was there the whole way with the 2011 Alabama title team. He'd transferred in to be the Crimson Tide's right tackle. But he never made it. This is the story of Douglas's short UA career, the impact he made, and the loss his family feels to this day.

You feel his presence in the well-appointed brick home on Snowshill Way: the ceiling, stretching skyward, seemingly designed to hold all 6'7" of Douglas. He's there in his mother's strength. Karla Douglas is the backbone of the family, a competitor who, when her world caved in, dug in and fought back.

You hear him in his late father's laugh. David Douglas battled demons for years after Aaron's death, up until his very own, but he bounced back for his family with that warmhearted chuckle. The dark days were behind him before his passing, so much so that he could see a future.

Aaron remains in his baby sister's face. Ashley Douglas looks like him, and she's growing like a weed, long legs and all, just like he did at the same age 15 years earlier.

The photos still hang on the walls. Captured for posterity's sake, the gentle giant walks hand in hand with his little sister down a dirt road on one wall, adjacent to a studio shot of the two, her atop his back. When she smiles, there he is.

The Freshman All–Southeastern Conference plaque sits in the basement just outside his room under a pile of awards, recognitions, and honors that he never made much of a fuss over.

Aaron Douglas is no longer here, and now neither is David. Yet Aaron remains a part of the UA football program. Especially in Tuscaloosa.

The Douglas family went through hell and back. Years after the death of their only son to an accidental drug overdose, Karla and David bounced back. Then Karla was left to keep fighting when David passed away nearly five years after his son died. This family remains close to my heart. I watched as Karla pulled her family through grief after Aaron died and watched her continue on after David succumbed to brain cancer. As a sportswriter, I watch athletes overcome adversity and fight through injury on a daily basis, but nothing is as brave to me, or has left such an impression on me, as an Alabama football player who never played a down for the Crimson Tide and his remarkable family. This is their story.

Aaron Douglas grew up in Knoxville, Tennessee, the firstborn of two proud University of Tennessee legacies. His father, David, played offensive guard for the Volunteers, winning an SEC championship in 1985, and his mom, Karla, was a forward on Pat Summitt's first national championship basketball team in 1987.

Aaron, a talented tight end and two-time Mr. Football honoree at Maryville High School, on the outskirts of Knoxville, committed to Tennessee before his junior year without ever taking a visit to another school. The matriculation to Rocky Top was never in doubt. When David and Karla were married in the mid-1980s, David's former offensive line coach, Phillip Fulmer, wrote the newlyweds a handwritten note: "Dear David, I'm sorry I wasn't able to make it to your wedding, but I certainly wish you and your new wife many years of happiness and love. May God bless you and yours. P.S. I've got the scholarship papers ready for the first boy."

That boy became the first commitment for Tennessee's 2008 class. After Douglas redshirted that year, new UT coach Lane Kiffin moved Aaron from tight end to right tackle. Accompanying the change was a new jersey number. "He called and told me, 'Pops, I'm getting your old number, No. 78.' I hung up and cried," David said.

Despite never having played the position, Aaron was named a Freshman All-American and Freshman All-SEC after starting 10 games in 2009.

His ability to excel on the field masked deep-seated problems, though. During his two years at Tennessee, Aaron was introduced to prescription pills by teammates, Karla said. He developed the habit of taking Adderall before practices and games to amp himself up and oxycodone, a powerful drug used to treat chronic pain, to bring himself down. "He smoked pot and drank in high school, but the pills started in college," Karla said.

The problem got so bad that Aaron admitted to his parents that he needed help, and Tennessee sent him to rehabilitation for three days. The ongoing temptations in Knoxville were too strong, though, and when Kiffin departed for Southern California, Aaron's resolve to leave the Volunteers program strengthened. New coach Derek Dooley made things a bit more difficult on the family when he stipulated that he would release Aaron to schools no closer than eight hours from home.

To a family whose son was struggling with addiction, that seemed unduly harsh. But they made it work. Aaron enrolled in Arizona Western College in Yuma, Arizona, and thrived. The distance from home and from temptation actually helped. He threw himself into writing and music. A love of hip-hop music fueled his desire to record his own songs. Back at the family home, he transformed his closet into a recording booth, complete with soundproofing foam. "It was a way to deal with whatever he was going through inside," Karla said. "He just liked taking his words and making music and putting them into what he felt."

Things were coming together for Aaron Douglas. A couple of years had gone sideways on him, but the gifted athlete seemed to be on the other side of his troubles when he got to Tuscaloosa in the spring of 2011. He was brought in to compete for the vacant left tackle position at Alabama, but the team ultimately moved Barrett Jones there, leaving Aaron to start at right tackle. He was doing well, too. All with a broken foot.

Aaron had broken his left foot in December 2009, during bowl preparations for Tennessee's Chick-fil-A Bowl game against Virginia Tech, but never told anyone about it. He kept playing on that foot. It wasn't until after spring practice concluded at Alabama in 2011 that it was finally addressed.

David got a call from then–Alabama offensive line coach Jeff Stoutland telling him something was wrong with Aaron. "I said, 'What's he told you?'" David said. "He said, 'Nothing.' I said, 'His right foot's broken and he won't tell anybody.' I called Aaron, and I'm reasoning with him that spring's over and that he needs to get this taken care of. He said, 'Pops, I can't do that. I've got to start.'" But he eventually did have an operation on the foot. David said, "When they performed the surgery, they took out two huge chunks of broken bone."

The foot surgery brought with it its own set of worries. How would Aaron handle the pain pills? Would he head down the addiction path again? Those fears were eased with help from the hands-on staff and trainers at Alabama. It was a group effort to keep an eye on him.

Despite the family's deep Tennessee roots, Aaron felt at home at UA. He thrived under Scott Cochran's intense workouts. The talent around him, the structure, the family atmosphere— all of it fit Aaron's competitiveness and temperament. "He was so happy there," Karla said. "I can remember him calling, it was during one of the workouts I guess in February, and him saying, 'I have never been around this many incredible athletes.' He said in February, 'We'll win the national championship.' He knew."

His family grew to love Tuscaloosa too. It began on the official visit in October 2010. "Just the atmosphere and the first-class people and the tradition, everything about it was just so comfortable and just so awesome that I think that whole rivalry thing went out the window," Karla said.

Ashley already had an Alabama cheerleader uniform ready for game days. David and Karla had their sights set on a condo within walking distance of Bryant-Denny Stadium. Aaron had gone 60–0 with four state championships in high school, and now the family was ready to experience two national championships.

Then it ended so quickly. It began so innocently, with a trip to visit family friends in Jacksonville, Florida, after the UA spring semester concluded in May 2011. Wanting to avoid the old temptations of Knoxville for a few days, Aaron opted for an impromptu mini-vacation. After dinner that Wednesday night with a friend, Aaron connected with two nursing students he'd met earlier that day on the beach. He'd told them he was an Alabama football player, but they didn't believe him. After looking him up on Google, they invited him to a party in Fernandina Beach, the county seat of Nassau County, about 25 miles northeast of Jacksonville. On the cab ride to the party, Aaron purchased 40-milligram methadone tablets from the cab driver, Rodney Young Odum. Aaron Douglas would never make it home.

He was last seen alive at 2:00 AM and was discovered face-down on the second-story balcony at 2570 First Avenue in Fernandina Beach at 8:13 AM on Thursday morning. The medical examiner's report listed the cause of death as "multiple drug toxicity" with methadone (pain pill), diazepam (valium), and carisoprodol (muscle relaxant) in his system. The coroner ruled it was the methadone tablets that killed him. First reports of his death surfaced on Twitter.

David received a phone call from Stoutland asking if he'd spoken with Aaron. Not wanting to upset the family until it was confirmed, Stoutland held off in relaying the news. A flurry of phone calls and texts to Aaron went unanswered before Karla called the police, which confirmed for her the tragic news. "It's an ongoing nightmare," Karla said. "What hurts so bad with Aaron is that I had seen him struggle with use and abuse. I had seen him at his lowest point, and when he was in Tuscaloosa, it just seemed like everything was falling into place and he had turned the corner. That's what hurt the most was just knowing how good he was doing and just making a fatal choice."

Odum was arrested in August 2011 and charged with manslaughter and the sale/delivery of a controlled substance. He pleaded guilty and was sentenced to 2 years in prison along with 2 years of house arrest and 10 years of probation following his time served. The 53-year-old Odom, a father of three, entered a Florida state prison on October 30, 2013, and was released on July 9, 2015. David harbored no ill will toward Odom, acknowledging there was no intent to kill his son. One day, he said, he'd like to meet him.

"I played in the NFL, and I thought I'd heard of everything there was, but pain pills? I didn't even have a clue," David said. "Why did we let him go down there?"

It was a whirlwind after that. Grief set in immediately for Karla, but David threw himself into work. He withdrew, swallowed the grief, and went into a deep depression. He drank too much beer, his weight ballooned, he quit taking care of himself. He stopped talking. A salesman by profession, David never had trouble communicating with people. That changed after Aaron died. "For all the years I've run my mouth, I couldn't talk to anybody. Not Karla, not my brother, not my dad, no one," David said. He turned his back on his faith. "I said, 'God, I want nothing to do with you,'" he said.

Karla forged ahead. It wasn't easy, but she knew there was a little girl at home who needed her. Aaron and Karla were alike in that way. Both had toughness. Aaron went two years without revealing to his coaches that he had a broken foot. Karla wrapped her family up tight and dragged them through the grief, refusing to stop living. She credits therapy, her faith, and teaching and coaching at Maryville High School for keeping her head above water.

Karla, who averaged 9.4 points and 7.7 rebounds during her Tennessee career, became an assistant basketball coach at the school. The game gave her something to pour herself into besides grief. "The first year it was hard, walking back into this school," she said, noting that Aaron's picture hung prominently just outside the gymnasium. "But people talk about him and remember him still. It's a good place to be."

Mother's Day is especially rough, and the second Sunday in May is often near the anniversary of Aaron's death. Birthdays aren't easy either. Aaron and Ashley share the same date of birth: September 19. The family, though, turned it into a positive. Rather than having it be a morose affair, the family celebrates with fireworks. Aaron's friends come over too, both to remember their best friend and for Ashley. "She remembers him picking her up by her ankles. It would be a carnival ride almost for her. Popping her toes. All the stuff big brothers do," Karla said. "We look at pictures. She remembers him. Aaron's friends have tried to be her big brother. It really means a lot. She's got three or four big brothers now."

Still, it is in the quiet moments that Karla misses him most, tripping over his size 17 shoes in the front doorway or his sprawling legs bumping against tables, accidentally knocking over a glass of tea. She especially misses receiving text messages from him. "What I miss the most are his hugs and his smile and his sense of humor," she said. "I don't know if people realize he was a funny, witty, off-the-wall kind of guy. He was just a goofy kid."

She also substitute teaches at the high school, which helps keep her close to young people, reminding her of Aaron.

A black notebook filled with handwritten notes by Aaron's friends is one of Karla's treasured possessions. Her fingers slowly trace over the words, reading memories of the young man she misses so much it hurts. She thumbs through it when she wants to feel close to her son. She had no idea that he had touched so many people's lives, especially at Alabama, where he only spent a few months.

"The thing that all people saw was the athlete—the big, tall, strong guy," she said. "I don't think they realized how sensitive and kind and compassionate he was. That might have been his biggest struggle, because here on the outside [he was] this big, huge giant and on the inside [he was] just mushy. The way he talked to his friends about his family, which makes me cry every time I think about it, some of these things you never know. I was so proud. I really didn't know. You hope and pray that your kid will have that kind of influence on somebody, but you really don't know." The local preschool planted a tree for Aaron, a red maple, in honor of the gentle giant.

There are boxes of Aaron's writings and his music that his mother flips through from time to time. His bedroom remains almost untouched. His Maryville jersey is spread out on the bed, waiting for him to come home. "I have dreams about him," Karla said. "At the time when I need him the most, he's there. He's standing in the background just grinning."

Things were much more difficult for David. He stopped watching football because it hurt too much. It took reaching a despair he didn't think possible for him to get up off of his knees. But he rebounded. The man in his mid-50s—who had played for five years in the NFL, including in the 1989 Super Bowl—had stopped watching football. But then he remembered that his favorite football memories were watching Aaron dominate on the high school field. So he threw himself back into the game. He visited Maryville High School practices again. He put his 1985 SEC championship ring back on his right hand.

Then he was diagnosed with grade 4 brain cancer in July 2013. It started with memory problems. Karla demanded that he go to the hospital. Tests revealed a pecan-sized tumor on his brain. Jimmy Sexton—Nick Saban's agent—got him in to see Dr. Henry Friedman at the Duke Cancer Center in Durham, North Carolina. David, drafted in the eighth round by the Cincinnati Bengals in 1986, was Sexton's first-ever football player signed to Athletic Resource Management. The surgery and treatments initially worked. The MRIs were clear. And then it returned. David ultimately passed away on February 27, 2016. It was all too cruel for Karla and Ashley. How much is a family expected to endure? But Karla rose again. For Ashley. For Aaron. For David.

The family established the Aaron Douglas Foundation, which presents two scholarships to Maryville High School students each year, one each for Aaron's two passions in life: athletics and music/fine arts. The goal is to help young people realize their dreams and warn of the dangers of prescription drugs by providing resources to children and families, all with the intent of keeping Aaron's memory alive. "We want to be able to share Aaron's story. At this age, they're all invincible in their mind," Karla said. "We want them to realize, 'No, you're not.'

"That's what I hope one of the things that the foundation can do is to make these kids realize that it just takes one bad choice."

But Aaron's legacy remains it Tuscaloosa. His celebration of life took place at Cokesbury United Methodist Church in Knoxville. The turnout overwhelmed the family. Three national championship head coaches sat with the family: Johnny Majors, Phillip Fulmer, and Nick Saban. Also on hand were Duke coach David Cutcliffe, then–UA director of athletics Mal Moore, and two planes full of Alabama players, staff, coaches, and administrators. The response from Alabama made an impression on David and Karla. "I turn around and there's the whole team, the whole coaching staff," David said. "Here

Alabama's just had the horrible tornado, and the players have all gone home, which meant they had to get their own way to Knoxville to that funeral. I'm going to say just about the whole team was there. It just floored me."

Alabama kept surprising too. After the Crimson Tide topped LSU in the BCS National Championship Game in January 2012, the Douglas family received a phone call. Saban made the decision to present the family with a national championship ring for Aaron. The ring arrived on May 11, 2012, the day before the one-year anniversary of Aaron's passing. His No. 77 was a helmet decal for the entire 2011 season. "That one's in the family safe deposit box," David said then.

Former Alabama teammates still keep in touch too. Cody Mandell, Daniel Geddes, and Austin Shepherd, who was Aaron's roommate, reach out via social media from time to time to check in on the family.

"Our family was UT, is UT," David said. "When Aaron went to 'Bama and he fell in love with that staff and those people and the school—people are what make schools great or not. I tell people now, 'Don't come back and tell me Alabama sucks. It's OK for you to be a Tennessee fan, but if you had someone who was going there and saw how great a job Nick Saban did, how great a person he was to those kids, then you wouldn't be talking this way.'"

Despite never playing a game for Alabama, Aaron Douglas is always there. On September 11, 2011, a portion of Aaron's remains were spread on the Alabama practice fields.

20

Damien Harris

IN HIS TWO SEASONS AS THE NEW ENGLAND PATRIOTS'
starting running back, Damien Harris has averaged 4.8 yards
per rush. That puts him into some pretty elite company and rare
air in the NFL. Alabama has served as a reliable farm system
of sorts for NFL franchises, but Harris's success as the lead
running back for the NFL's most elite franchise has come as a
bit of a surprise.

Not because Harris isn't talented. He's certainly that. But he
never had the type of season that Derrick Henry or Najee Harris
had when they were the lead backs during their Crimson Tide
careers. To be fair, though, Harris never got as many carries as
those guys. His season high for rushes during his career was
150. And with those carries, he did the most, averaging 6.0
yards per carry throughout his four-year career.

His success in the NFL came after essentially not playing his
rookie season in 2019. He played in only two games and rushed

the ball just four times. But he emerged in 2020 and 2021 with a combined 339 carries for 1,632 yards and 17 touchdowns, including 15 rushing touchdowns in 2021, which ranked tied for the second in the NFL. He's become a dependable part of the Patriots offense.

He waited his turn at Alabama too. He got only 46 carries his freshman season in 2015. He was playing behind the Heisman Trophy winner that year, but it was surprising at the time that he didn't take some of the load off Henry, who rushed the ball 395 times that season. Still, his career worked out.

It was at Alabama that Harris showed his personality as well. Alabama players don't often show a lot during press availability, where they are coached to give the safest answers possible. Harris still colored in between the lines in that regard, but he managed to show who he was at the same time.

His ability to make friends and fit into any situation is a gift some are born with. Harris certainly was. That ability started at a young age. When he was a little boy, he would fling himself off the wooden pew inside Goodloe's Chapel Baptist Church—sucking on the two middle fingers on his left hand—and search for a hand to shake. He'd start with the pastor, then press palms with the deacons all along the way to nearly everyone in the church. Eventually, every week, he'd find himself in front of the same lady. She didn't like children, but the little boy stopped in front of her every Sunday, smiled at her, and put his hand on her knee.

For nearly two years she ignored him, as she was wont to do with children. But that never deterred him. One day he broke her. She smiled back, scooped him up on her lap, and the two had a conversation—the first of many. When Harris now goes back to his church in Richmond, Kentucky, she can't wait to see him. When he's not there, she frequently asks Harris's mom,

Lynn, how her favorite boy is. "He's always had that ability to overcome anything that might prevent people from being friends," Lynn Harris said. "He's always been able to be friendly with people."

That's the essence of Harris, who became best friends in college with a backup quarterback who's now the starting quarterback at New England: Mac Jones. Harris jokingly called him his son back at Alabama, and the pair remains close today. Harris has a free-flowing personality that easily connects with others, even those from affluent backgrounds. He's been spotted in Boston with movie star Mark Wahlberg, and he's rubbed elbows with the owner of the Patriots, Robert Kraft.

But that personality definitely has a don't-tread-on-me aspect. He is true to himself even when met with rudeness or obstinance.

It's hard to describe, but Harris was never the superstar in college that some running backs were. You can't really put your finger on it, but he just didn't have the same cachet. The same guy who quietly led the team in rushing was the same guy who blocked a punt against Florida State in the season opener in 2017 and scored a rushing touchdown in the Crimson Tide's first four games of the season that year. He did so without a lot of fanfare. He was often overlooked for the newer or shinier toy in Alabama's loaded offensive toy chest. Still, all he did was make plays.

Spend any time with him and he'd be a thoughtful young man—when he wanted to be. If he wasn't in the mood, though, he could be downright surly. You never knew which Harris you were going to get. When he was thoughtful, you quickly learned that his success on the football field didn't make the man. The skill that brought him from eastern Kentucky to Tuscaloosa, the same artistry that made him the top-ranked prep running back in the nation, was only a part of his identity. Football didn't define Damien Harris. His thoughtfulness and personality did.

In a political climate that was particularly divisive, Harris was never afraid to voice his opinion. As you'd expect, those thoughts weren't always welcomed, and oftentimes he was met with "Just run the football" responses during his four years at UA. That negativity didn't stop him from wading into those waters. It was something teammates never dared take on, and probably for good reason. Alabama players go through extensive media training and are taught to steer clear of controversial topics. That could be abstaining from trash talk and certainly would include avoiding things outside of football. But when topics arose on social media that Harris was passionate about, he talked about them. He was often told to stick to football by fans who didn't want their running back to speak on such things. But sticking to sports was never an option for Harris. "Football does not define me, sir. It is just a platform to help me achieve my dreams both on and off the field," Harris once tweeted in response to a hater.

Harris was great at football long before he landed in Tuscaloosa. His coaching staff at Madison Southern High School realized quickly that he was the best player they had during his first scrimmage his freshman year. "Our varsity guys weren't the best, and we were really scrambling to find players at certain positions," Harris's running backs coach, Byron Smoot, said. "We thought, 'Let's give this freshman a chance.' Damien got in the game. The first pitch we gave him he [took]...about 75 yards for a touchdown. We started looking at each other. It was like watching college football where you see the defense have angles on individuals and the individual will just burst and accelerate past them. That's really the first time we looked at each other like, 'This kid is special.' We knew then we had to start rethinking our offensive strategy and how we were going to develop him."

As his career progressed, it became more and more obvious Harris's talent would give him a bevy of college choices. For the longest time, his mom couldn't wrap her head around it. She was one of the main reasons Harris chose Madison Southern over Madison Central, where he was originally zoned. The family didn't like the direction of the program at Madison Central. Lynn Harris actually thought of uprooting the family to Lexington to give her son more opportunities to be successful and get noticed. However, she couldn't afford it. Instead they took a leap of faith and went to Madison Southern under the direction of first-year coach Jon Clark. It worked out for both parties.

Even as her son was becoming a star, Lynn never let herself believe it was true. "Where we're from, the chances of ending up at a University of Alabama are probably slim to none," she said. "I never thought [he] would get to where he is right now. I thought he might be good enough to play for [Eastern Kentucky]. The University of Alabama? I'm still in shock. He's a junior, and I'm still in shock. Sometimes I have to say, 'That's really my son.' It's like I have to pinch myself sometimes."

When the scholarship offers came pouring in, it was Harris's ability to stay true to who he was that gave him the confidence to leave his home state and go to Alabama. There was pressure to go to Kentucky. Programs used Alabama's running backs depth to argue against it: "Why go to Alabama? You'll never be the man there. You'll never get all the carries there." Those ideas may have planted insecurities in other recruits' minds, but the headstrong Harris never saw it the same way. "Whenever I chose Alabama, I didn't really think about that," Harris said. "People say, 'If you're going to play, you're going to play." It doesn't matter who's there, who you have to compete with. It's just if you're ready to play, if you're capable of playing, you're going to play. So I wasn't really worried about that. But being there, I saw it as more of an advantage than a disadvantage. A lot of people think it takes away from how many carries you get or how many yards you potentially get or how much attention you get from being the premier guy at a program like Alabama, but I think that it helps you in the long run, because it's a long season. Over the course of 14, 15 games throughout the course of a long season, it's nice to have guys come in and split reps with you and split time with you. It keeps you from getting banged up. It keeps you from being tired and worn down throughout the year. I kind of think that's one of the advantages of having a lot of guys."

Groupthink has never been a trap for Harris. He's a free thinker, even when it's not convenient for him to be one. That's how he ended up at Alabama instead of staying in Kentucky, even with all the pressure surrounding him to do so. He had the stubbornness to do what he wanted and not go with the crowd in high school.

Once during a high school basketball game between Harris's school, Madison Southern, and Madison Central, Harris decided to sit with his cousin, who attended Madison Central. Basketball isn't taken lightly in Kentucky, especially considering the rivalry between the two schools, and the star running back's act of sitting with his cousin in the other school's section caused somewhat of a stir at his high school. Silly as that might sound, it's true. But those who knew Harris best didn't think twice about it. "It wasn't that he was cheering against Southern. He was just real close with his cousin Nick, and so he sat with Nick and talked and they played around, and I think some people really got upset by it," Smoot said.

"When you start thinking about who Damien is and know who Damien is, there was no ill will about doing that. He just went over there, and it was a chance that he got to spend some time with his cousin, and he did."

That independence was something he applied throughout every aspect of his life at Alabama. He moved through social circles with ease, and that was why he was able to become fast friends with Jones. He was also close with star linebacker Rashaan Evans, now with the Atlanta Falcons. Color didn't matter to him. Neither did socioeconomic status. He could be friends with all. When he first arrived at Alabama, it wasn't uncommon to find him at a traditionally white fraternity house for a party. But when it came time to find a fraternity of his own, he pledged Omega Psi Phi, a historically African American fraternity.

"He didn't talk to me very much during that time because he wanted to be grown about this and go through it," Lynn Harris said. "It's difficult. It's a difficult process. They have to go through a lot. They have a lot of demands placed on them. Once he came through it, he was a different person. His maturity had gone up some. His mindset was different. The way he looked at things was different. He learned a lot. They taught him a lot. He takes great pride in that fraternity, and I'm proud of him for it."

It's a source of pride for Harris. He's often seen in his fraternity shirt, and when he scored his first touchdown of the season against Florida State in 2017, he threw the hooks up, which is a signature hand gesture that originated from Omega Psi Phi. "Being a part of Omega Psi Phi fraternity is something I hold dearly to me just as much as football, just as much as life outside of football," Harris said. "There's so many connections within the fraternity just like with football. There's a lot of similarities between fraternities and football. They're both a bond of brotherhood, people that you meet and you'll carry on friendships for the rest of your life."

To those who know him, it's not surprising he moves around so effortlessly from one social circle to the next. It all goes back to his personal motto: "If you're cool with me, then I'm cool with you." Harris is just as comfortable around white people as he is Black. It's how he was raised, and it's who he is. "When he enrolled at Southern, I think there were four, maybe five, Black kids there," Lynn Harris said. "It was also a school known for racial tension as well. I told him, 'We'll tackle it head-on, we'll be a united front and we'll handle it.' He trusted me, and we rode with it. Where we're from is predominantly white, but Damien, he's never been one to look at...race. Even as a freshman and sophomore at Alabama, he's had...Keaton Anderson, Richie Petitbon, Hale Hentges—he hung out with all of them. That's his group. That's one of his main groups of friends. Then he turns around and pledges Omega Psi Phi, and he has that group of friends. And he goes back and forth hanging with everybody. He's a social butterfly. He likes to have a good time and surround himself with good people."

The standard definition of success for an Alabama football player is an NFL career, and Nick Saban puts his players into the league with regularity. That's just reality for the best college football program in the nation. Harris never allowed his draft status to define him. He was going to be happy if he made it in the NFL or not. He was drafted in the third round, a spot where players are expected to make a contribution for their teams in their first contract. After a first year in which he wasn't involved much, Harris again was never going to let himself be defined by whether he carried a football for money or not. "Making it to the NFL and earning lots of money would be great and all that, but it would be unrealistic to make that my only goal," he said.

"One thing that I've always joked around about—I've been to the Bahamas a few times now. I went once for spring break my freshman year and I've been back. I always tell myself if I get to the point in my life where I can go to the Bahamas whenever I want, then I'll consider myself successful."

And he knew he didn't need to play football to do that. But things changed in his second season with the Patriots. He carried the ball more. Then he had his sort of breakout season in 2021, rushing for those 15 touchdowns. That put him in elite company in the NFL. But Harris knows a career in the sport he loves is fleeting, that it'll encompass only a small portion of his life. That perspective shapes his current reality and is why he's never let himself buy into the fact that he's any different from anyone else just because he's good at a sport. "Football is going to end one day," Harris said. "Everybody says that, but I don't think everyone truly grasps the concept. Sometimes I think people that watch football...think that's all that our lives consist of, which right now it consumes a good amount of your attention, your focus, what you do every day. That's true. But in the grand scheme of life, you play football for maybe 20 years of your life if you're a great player. That's if you make it for a couple of years in the league, which doesn't happen very often. That's another 50 to 60 years of life that you still have to live. It's kind of like, once football is over, then what?

"Football's a great game. Sports are great for people. But that's not your whole life. There's a lot to look forward to after that."

21

T. J. Yeldon

ALABAMA HAS RESET THE BAR AT RUNNING BACK IN THE NICK Saban era. The team has produced the only two running backs to win the Heisman Trophy since Reggie Bush won the sport's top individual honor in 2005. Because of that, other Crimson Tide running backs—truly great ones, at that—probably haven't received the appreciation they deserve.

Timothy Yeldon—known to all as T. J.—fits into that category. Had he returned for his senior season, he'd lead the program in career rushing yards. As it stands, he ranks fifth in the program's career rushing touchdowns with 37. He got swallowed up by the great backs before him, those who were there at the start of his career, and one who emerged at the end of his career. So there remains something to be said for T. J. Yeldon.

Truth be told, there's a lot remaining to be said for and about the University of Alabama's more enigmatic and underappreciated players who'd just as soon run through a patch of saw briars as stand in front of a camera or a microphone and answer questions in which they see no value. Yeldon is a bit of an introvert in front of the media. For that, and a multitude of other reasons, Yeldon remains one of the most unassuming and minimized stars in the Crimson Tide's vast history.

For those who appreciate history and for those who recognize greatness, Alabama fans would be wise to show some love to Yeldon, who—despite production that puts him with the greats in school history—somehow fails to receive his due for a variety of factors. During his career Yeldon was the bike in the backyard—solid and reliable even after years of use—while everyone stares longingly at the wrapped, unknown, and unproven shiny new ride under the tree.

As a freshman in 2012, Yeldon got a bit of shine, rushing for more yards than any true freshman running back ever at Alabama. Even then, though, he was behind Eddie Lacy, a gifted back who would go on to win NFL Rookie of the Year. A year later it was Yeldon's show, but fans and media couldn't contain their excitement, anxious to get a peek at what then-freshman jumbo back Derrick Henry had under the hood. That continued, and for good reason, because as we know now, Henry was special.

Even as Yeldon set his sights on a career rushing record going into his junior year, the focus seemed to skip over Yeldon onto Henry and turbocharged backfield mate Kenyan Drake. That year was the only year Yeldon didn't reach 1,000 yards rushing.

It's time to appreciate what Yeldon accomplished during his three years at Alabama. He arrived in Tuscaloosa via Daphne, Alabama, a town situated nearly halfway in between Spanish Fort and Fairhope in Baldwin County and just across the bay from Mobile. As a senior at Daphne High School, playing for the Trojans, Yeldon was a prodigy. Always bigger and stronger than his classmates, he thrived in athletics, especially football. He adeptly crossed over between quarterback, wide receiver, in the Wildcat, and as a running back.

When his freshman football season ended, Daphne coach Glenn Vickery promoted him to the varsity, where he found a home as a slot receiver. In one of his first games with the big boys, Yeldon returned a kickoff 99 yards against a good Pace (Florida) High School team. Vickery knew he was witnessing something special. "He was always what I'd say is ahead of his time—athletically, physically, maturity-wise," Vickery said. "You could always see the potential that he had the ability to be a great player. T. J. was always the kind of kid that carried himself well."

A great deal of his high school career was spent at wide receiver. "If the ball was in the area, T. J. was going to catch it," Vickery said. "He was bigger and stronger than most DBs. If there was a jump ball, he was going to win it."

The Trojans won a Class 6A state championship in 2010, beating the powerhouse Hoover Buccaneers by a score of 7–6 and snapping the Bucs' 21-game winning streak. Yeldon scored the only touchdown for Daphne. It came out of the Wildcat. "He was a very versatile player for us," Vickery joked.

That led to a senior season for the ages in which Yeldon rushed for 2,193 yards and 31 touchdowns, outdueling Hueytown's Jameis Winston for Mr. Football honors. It was the first time a running back had taken home the award since 2000, when Carnell Williams did so. He averaged nearly 10 yards per carry that season. All the major colleges came calling, but it was Auburn that got his commitment. "I had a good relationships with the coaches—Coach [Curtis] Luper, Coach [Gene] Chizik,

Coach [Gus] Malzahn before he left," Yeldon said. "I felt kind of comfortable there, but then they all started leaving."

What happened next remains a source of contention. Yeldon spurned his verbal commitment to Auburn and opted for Alabama, waiting until the coaching dead period in the recruiting calendar to do so. Yeldon was an early enrollee, essentially assuring that no Auburn coaches could contact him before he enrolled for the spring semester at Alabama in 2012. It was a simple decision. It was a business decision. "Just the running backs here, the tradition of running backs at Alabama," Yeldon said. "They all had a good time here, played their years, and they accomplished a lot of goals they had and got drafted. That's why I wanted to come here."

There wasn't much of an adjustment to major college football. During the A-Day spring game in 2012, Yeldon announced his presence with 179 all-purpose yards. He caught 5 passes for 91 yards, including a 50-yard touchdown, and added 88 yards on 16 carries rushing to earn the Dixie Howell Most Valuable Player of the Game Award. When the real games started, it didn't seem much of a challenge either.

Yeldon hit the ground running with a breakout 111-yard, 1-touchdown performance against Michigan in his first collegiate game. That performance caught the attention of Mark Ingram Jr., who was with the New Orleans Saints, who tweeted his appreciation for the freshman's game that day. The season wasn't much different, as he posted five 100-yard rushing games, despite playing behind Lacy, on the way to 1,108 yards and 12 rushing touchdowns. It was the first time an Alabama true freshman had run for 1,000 yards.

Despite his overall body of work, Yeldon's Alabama career is and will likely always be defined by one play: the screen against LSU in Death Valley. It was a game of flipped emotions.

A Yeldon third-quarter fumble at the LSU 10-yard line cost Alabama points. For a moment or two, he couldn't shake it. With the game winding down and Alabama trailing 17–14, he made amends, catching a screen pass from quarterback AJ McCarron and racing 28 yards untouched for the game-winning touchdown.

As he crossed the goal line, Yeldon reached the ball out a bit with his right hand, readjusted, and flexed his arms together multiple times while letting out a primal scream. It's the most emotion Yeldon showed on a football field while running the ball for the Crimson Tide.

Vickery was at UAB Hospital in Birmingham following major surgery when Yeldon scored. Drifting in and out of sleep, he awakened from bed with his wife screaming. "I was on some pretty strong medicine, and my wife woke up the entire hospital screaming, 'T. J. scored!'" Vickery said. "I saw the emotion he showed, and you could tell how much that meant to him. But that's about the most you're going to get from him."

Yeldon was a man of mystery around the Alabama football complex. Not to his teammates or coaches but to reporters. Despite a stellar legacy he rarely did interviews. It just was not who he was. "I just don't think it's a good idea to talk to the media," Yeldon said in a rare one-on-one interview while at Alabama. "I just don't like doing it. Not my personality, not at all."

To hear his family tell it, it's been that way for a while. He's the same back home in Daphne. When visitors come to the family home, Yeldon retreats to his room. "He doesn't do a lot of talking," his mother, Kimberly Yeldon, said. "Me and his dad are the same way. We don't really talk to a lot of people. We're quiet too."

Kimberly and T. J.'s father, Timothy Yeldon Sr., missed just one of their youngest son's football games at Alabama, a road game at Missouri in 2012, T. J.'s freshman season. To honor his parents that day, T. J. wore a wristband during the game with the words KIM AND TIM written in black marker.

He was reserved around his parents too, albeit to a lesser degree. Except for that one time when his parents surprised him with his first car during his sophomore year in 2013. "We got him a Tahoe, and we drove up to his dorm room and we parked on the side of the dorm, and we told him we were downstairs. He came down and he was looking around and looking around and said, 'I don't see y'all.' We told him, 'We're right here in the truck,' and he started smiling from ear to ear. He was so excited. We told him to get in and drive us somewhere." That was about the extent of emotion you'd see publicly from T. J. Yeldon.

His legacy is set at Alabama, but it's an underrated one. He just gets lost among all the quality backs the program has had. It's not fair, but that's what happens when you recruit the level of athlete UA does. Look at the career rushing list at Alabama, and you'll see what I'm talking about. Yeldon currently ranks sixth behind Najee Harris, Derrick Henry, Shaun Alexander, Bobby Humphrey, and Ken Darby.

His 5.8 career yards per carry average also ranks tied for fourth in program history (among rushers with a minimum of 400 carries), and his 37 career rushing touchdowns are fifth in school history. Yet Yeldon still doesn't get the love he deserves because of who came before and after him. His name doesn't get mentioned as much as Ingram's or Henry's or Drake's or Harris's. Vickery likens it to another Alabama player who he says went undervalued by Crimson Tide fans. "To me, and I go back a long way, the same thing happened to Alabama fans with Walter Lewis," Vickery said. "I think us smart people understood the value of Walter Lewis to that football team back in the day. The smart Alabama fans understand the value of T. J. Yeldon."

Some questioned Yeldon's fumbling problems, which sometimes were untimely. Vickery didn't want to hear that. "Somebody popped off to me the other day about T. J. fumbling, and I said, 'Look, when you break it down, he's rushed for over a mile. You couldn't carry a football a mile without dropping it seven times,'" Vickery said. "When SEC West guys hit you, you're going to fumble a couple of times."

But his teammates and coaches always gave thanks to Yeldon. They noticed the uncanny vision he possessed, the ability to cut back and make defenders miss, the skill to press the hole and set up his blocks. Perhaps UA coach Nick Saban said it best when he praised Yeldon's assets that often went unnoticed. "He has been by far, in my opinion, our most effective guy all the way around when it comes to blocking, running the ball, being a pass receiver, and I think I've said this before: people don't appreciate that in a running back, the things they do when they don't have the ball," Saban said. "Everybody sort of recognizes what they do when they do have it. And that's the part of it that has made him most effective."

Yeldon should be remembered for his career—and that certainly includes his screen pass touchdown to beat LSU—but he should definitely be remembered for more than that too.

22

Minkah Fitzpatrick

HE'S OFTEN USED AS AN EXAMPLE TO YOUNG FOOTBALL players who come to Alabama thinking they're ready to play right away. There's a difference between thinking you're ready and actually being ready. The difference between the two is up to the player. It takes ability, knowing the playbook, and the right mindset. Minkah Fitzpatrick had the right stuff in that regard.

Talent usually isn't the issue if Alabama recruits a player. That's a prerequisite. That doesn't mean that he doesn't need to be developed. Depending on the position, sometimes a player needs to be physically developed. If you play near the line of scrimmage, weight and strength must be added, especially for offensive and defensive linemen. A Crimson Tide player must also be developed mentally. Competitive character, the ability to focus not on the past or the future but the now, is necessary to play for Nick Saban.

That's where the rubber meets the road in terms of players actually being ready to suit up and play for Saban. Some positions are easier to do that in than others. Running backs and wide receivers have an easier path to the field than, say, defensive backs. Especially in Saban's complex system. That's what makes it all the more impressive that Fitzpatrick did what he did in his first year in the Alabama program. He played in all 14 games his freshman campaign and had two interception returns for touchdowns.

Fitzpatrick showed what he could do on the field when he first got to campus. It was how he conducted himself off the field that sewed up the job for him. If you're looking to explain what made Fitzpatrick such a valuable, difference-making player to the nation's No. 1 team, it's important to look off the field as much as you do on it.

You could start with the example of how during a bye week of his junior year, the first thing the native New Jerseyan did upon returning to campus was study film. Or you could point to his attitude and aptitude in how he scored closer on a personality test than any other player in the Nick Saban era to the irascible head coach.

Or perhaps you could point to this story, which predates his Alabama days. During Fitzpatrick's senior year of high school, he spent his spring break not at the Jersey Shore or a sugar-sand locale on the Gulf Coast or even in the Florida hotbed of spring breakers. Instead, he spent the week on the sideline of Alabama's practice fields, studying the Crimson Tide's defense as the team underwent spring practice.

It's just an example of the mental makeup that prepared Fitzpatrick to take the field so early in his career. He made the sacrifices necessary to eventually earn the opportunities that he sought. He was always special that way. "I realized that coming to Alabama is serious," Fitzpatrick said. "I just wanted to be ahead of the game when I got here. I didn't want to be equal or I didn't want to be behind. So I came down here. I was learning the playbook. I was asking questions, following people around. So when I came in, it was a smooth transition."

The decision, rare for a teenager, was noticed by then–Alabama players. "I was here because I'm a little older than him. He watched us his whole spring break," former Crimson Tide cornerback Anthony Averett said. "I just remember when I was in high school, I wasn't thinking about football on spring break, and I was committed here. After seeing that, I saw that he's different. He's all football."

It was the beginning of the newcomer turning veterans' heads. At first, it was, "Look how good this freshman is. He can play." Then it turned into everyone judging their play and effort by Fitzpatrick's. Take his 2015 recruiting classmate, Damien Harris. In his own right, the junior running back was one the best backs in the SEC and the nation. A five-star player out of Kentucky, Harris judged himself against Fitzpatrick, his former roommate, for a long time. Players have a way of watching what the best players on the team do. They take their lead in how hard they work. In that way, Alabama players were always watching Fitzpatrick, a talented player to be sure but also one of its hardest workers.

"We came in at the same time, that summer our freshman year. Watching him during workouts, conditioning in the mornings and seven-on-seven, you would hear the older guys saying, 'Man, this kid is good,'" Harris said. "It was easy for us to say that because we were in the same class, but when I witnessed the older players like Reggie [Ragland], Tim [Williams], Reuben [Foster], Cyrus [Jones], Eddie [Jackson], all those guys on the defense, guys talking about how good he was, it was kind of eye-opening. He's that good. We'd been there maybe a month or so, and everybody was already talking about how good he was."

Going into their junior season, wanting to take his game to the next level, Harris set a goal for himself each week that revolved around Fitzpatrick. "We would do our summer workouts in the morning, conditioning, drills and stuff, and Minkah's always in the front of the line," Harris said. "I wanted to get better, so I told myself, 'I'm going to get in the first line. No matter who's in the front, I'm getting in the front line.' Because I knew Minkah [was] going to be up there. Every time we would do a drill, every time we would do a sprint, no matter what it was, halfway through the drill I would look to my right or my left and I would see how much farther ahead he was. And each week, I told myself I would get closer and closer and closer. For me, I was trying to get better, but I guess you could look at it as like that's how people see Minkah. They see him as someone to look up to, somebody you can identify as, 'This is the way things need to be done.' Guys look at him that way. Every time anybody sees Minkah do something, they say, 'I want to be like that guy.'"

It was that way from the day he got there. He was easy to spot. You would always see him before you heard him. Some players talk a good game, and that's where it ends. Fitzpatrick was always the opposite. You would see him working, and that was the example, not how loudly he was talking. He was fine with that. He preferred working in the background and not being the center of attention. It's funny, then, that that work is what put him in the spotlight. It's a place he eventually got used to, even if he didn't necessarily seek it out.

It can be nearly impossible for a player of Fitzpatrick's ilk to avoid the attention. These days simply avoiding the television or websites that state how good you are isn't enough. The articles get sent directly to athlete's phones. There's social media. It's really almost impossible for them to avoid it. Fitzpatrick did downplay it, though. Even compliments from his head coach didn't really faze him. He appreciated them, but they didn't mean that much to him.

But there were a couple people from whom positive words about his play did resonate: his parents. Minkah Sr. and Melissa, Minkah's parents, were set up by an uncle on his father's side. His mom, a natural athlete who never really participated in organized sports, and his dad, a football and basketball player, have been together ever since. They've seen their son play at a high level for a long time. So it can take a lot to impress them. "They're really hard on me, but only in sports," Fitzpatrick said. "It was a kind of tough love when it comes to football. My mother always gives me a grade after every game. She's given me an A like one or two times. We get grades here too, and I get an A like almost every other week. My mother's like, 'B- or a C+.' I say, 'Come on, Mom.' She knows how good I can be. She knows a lot about football too. She knows when I mess up and do little things that some people may not see. Hearing a compliment from my mother or father is a big deal."

Fitzpatrick's importance was undeniable for an Alabama team in his final year in 2017. The No. 1–ranked defense was riddled with injuries all season long. The linebacking corps was a walking MASH unit at some points during the season. As Fitzpatrick lay on the turf inside Bryant-Denny Stadium on two separate occasions during the Saturday night game against LSU, crimson-wearing fans all over the country held their collective breath. Some immediately declared the season over, the type of overreaction that was understandable when it seemed an entire linebacking group had suffered season-ending injuries. The Crimson Tide had been bitten by the long bug, and so every time a player went down, it was naturally assumed they'd suffered a season-ending injury.

Thankfully for the Alabama faithful, Minkah Fitzpatrick's hamstring and head/neck injuries weren't serious. The point remained, though, that the specter of Alabama having to play an extended amount of time without Fitzpatrick served as nightmare fuel for the Crimson Tide. Even in Fitzpatrick's limited absence against LSU—he missed a few series—what followed showed unequivocally the junior defensive back was UA's most valuable player. An injured Fitzpatrick equaled multiple player losses in the secondary. The majority of the time he played the Star defensive back position, but he also played Money in the dime, and if need be he lined up at safety and cornerback too. The thought of losing him from the defense was more than it could have handled.

His versatility was irreplaceable. It allowed him to broaden his game, which made him valuable for the next year's draft. His role in the dime defense gave him more opportunities to rush the quarterback in 2017. His eight tackles for loss that season ranked third on the team behind eventual first-round linebacker Rashaan Evans and second-round defensive lineman Raekwon Davis.

When senior linebacker Shaun Dion Hamilton was lost for the season due to injury, Fitzpatrick's responsibilities increased even more. He assumed more of the role of helping communicate the defense to the entire team from play to play. That's where his mental acumen and preparation to learn the defense so thoroughly years before paid off. And he built on that knowledge each season. That allowed him to play all those different positions.

"[He's] like playing with a mini-Saban," Averett said. "Having that in your secondary, to have that laser focus that Saban has, it makes things a lot easier, especially when it comes to communication across the board."

Before every practice Fitzpatrick listened to his position coach, Derrick Ansley, ask the same question: "Who are you going to affect today?" It's that message he tried to respond to. "I try to go out there and affect as many people as I can in a positive way," he said.

In that regard, it worked. Nearly everyone watched Minkah Fitzpatrick. Those who wanted to be the best judged themselves against the best. "Anytime I'm not on the field and Minkah's on the field, I'm always watching him," Harris said.

23

Eddie Jackson

ONE OF THE MORE PAINFUL YET OFTEN OVERLOOKED PARTS of the 2016 season was the injury to Eddie Jackson. That team was so dominant that one could almost forget that Jackson broke his leg on a punt return during the eighth game of the season.

On a great list of what-ifs, Alabama really could've used Jackson in the Clemson game for the national championship. It was a historically great defense that year, and his absence gets overlooked because the team continued on, but it definitely missed him, especially in that game.

His talents have revealed how good he is in the NFL. Drafted in the fourth round by the Chicago Bears, he has been a two-time Pro Bowler and a onetime member of the All-Pro team. That's never surprised Alabama fans, who recognized how good of an athlete he was in Tuscaloosa. He was a playmaker as a punt returner on top of his safety duties. The crazy story is how close none of it came to being.

Jackson came shockingly close to never playing major college football at all. Heck, he almost never played high school football either. He didn't take his classwork seriously, and he wasn't eligible to play in his first three seasons of high school because of grade issues. While his best friends made Parade All-America lists and took part in the Under Armour All-America Game, Jackson stewed in the background, under the radar to all except those in the know. What makes it all the sweeter now is that he became the first in his family to earn a college degree on top of being a great football player. In some ways, that means a lot more to him.

No example is greater to show how far Jackson traveled from high school through his college career than the 2016 season-opening blowout win over Southern Cal, when Jackson got caught up in the maelstrom on the sideline when sophomore safety Ronnie Harrison lost his cool, letting his emotions get the best of him. When Jackson told his safety running mate to calm down, Harrison screamed at Jackson through and around players. It was chaotic.

Perhaps Nick Saban said it best when describing what happened when he said: "I think the lesson to be learned is that when you have a teammate who is caring about you and trying to help you, the response should be 'Thank you,' not 'Screw you.'"

There was a time in his life, not too terribly long before, when Jackson might have been on the other end of that exchange. It wasn't hard for those who knew him best to imagine Jackson losing his cool and escalating the situation. That time had passed, though. He became the guy counseling younger players on the virtues of overcoming adversity rather than drowning in it.

Overcoming adversity wasn't new to Jackson. It was precisely how he'd come so far. His freshman season he lined up incorrectly and stretched with the offensive linemen, earning the ridicule of Saban on national television during a CBS *60 Minutes* broadcast. Then there was his sophomore year in the Iron Bowl, when he was repeatedly torched by Auburn for big play after big play. But Jackson didn't flinch. He only grew.

He switched from cornerback to safety in 2015, a decision the coaching staff implemented to get faster and more versatile on defense, and it paid off like a winning slot machine. Jackson tied for the league lead in interceptions with six that season. "How did I get here? It's really just fighting and pushing through things," Jackson said. "It gets hard here, it's tough. Some guys, they don't have the mental intensity for things, so they give up or they quit or stop. You just have to overcome everything.

"There were times when I thought I didn't know it was going to be this hard. You just have to keep fighting. I tell the young guys all the time, 'Coach Saban yells at you because he sees something in you. Just take the coaching, take all of it, and don't feel bad and don't take it personally. He's just doing it to help you.'"

That inner drive comes from his family—Angela Jackson, his mother, and Eddie Jackson II, his father. They never let their son believe he wasn't capable of achieving his dreams. He has a tattoo on his forearm that read TOUGH TIMES DON'T LAST. TOUGH PEOPLE DO. "It's something I live by," he said. "Depending on how tough you are, you can overcome anything."

In high school he had a grade-point average that fluctuated from 1.2 to 1.5, and Jackson was headed down a path of wasted potential. It was something he was familiar with, watching his older brother go through the same exact thing. Demar Dorsey was a star high school football player in South Florida, rated the No. 1 safety in the country in the recruiting class of 2010. Dorsey verbally committed to Michigan, but his plans were derailed when he didn't qualify academically. It's the same path Jackson was headed down. "I think he learned a lot from watching what his brother went through," Jackson II said. "Things to do and what not to do."

Yet there he was making the same mistakes as his brother. He watched his good friend and teammate at Northeast High School Stacy Coley (later a senior standout wide receiver at Miami who had a brief NFL career) get the recognition Jackson felt he also deserved. Only he wasn't eligible to play.

Then he transferred to Boyd Anderson High School, met Coach Wayne Blair, and slowly began to make progress in the classroom, helping pave the way for him to get on the field. "His older brother, that was the turning point," Blair said. "He got to see it at home. I always used to ask him, 'Do you want that same situation for yourself?' Between me and his father, I know that we utilized the same things. I piggybacked off of Eddie Sr."

Once he was on the field, Eddie's talent was obvious. In his first action, a jamboree game, he intercepted nationally ranked Tampa-Plant twice. He earned the nicknames Action Jackson and Super Eddie for the way he could summon his ability when it mattered most. Still, there were moments when the coaching staff played mind games with Jackson to help him reach his full potential. "Me and his position coach, Dwight McKenzie, we always used to have to put a carrot in his face in the sense that getting him ready for game time and making him feel like situations were worse than they were in order to get the best possible performance out of him," Blair said. "One time we sat him for two quarters of a game just so we could get Super Eddie to show up. And sure enough, Super Eddie did show up. Those were the little head games that me and Coach McKenzie had to play with young Mr. Jackson at the time."

So what did Super Eddie look like? During the playoffs his senior season, Jackson's grandmother passed. The team excused him and didn't expect him to play. Hours after the wake, Jackson showed up just prior to kickoff. "He put in over 180-something yards receiving, [and] he had one interception and also a punt return for a touchdown," Blair said. "So, Super Eddie."

Alabama began recruiting Jackson at the end of his final prep regular season, two games before the playoffs. His talents were so immense that even though he was late on the recruiting scene, all the big schools came calling, including UA, Florida State, and LSU. Alabama ultimately won out because Angela Jackson adored Saban. "My mom, she loved Coach Saban," Jackson said. "She's a big Saban fan.

"Probably because when he came in he wasn't talking about football. He was talking about school things. He wants you to be a better person on and off the field. Getting your degree and things like that."

On that front, Jackson held up his end of the bargain. He was contemplating entering the NFL Draft after his standout junior season, but he listened to his parents and Saban and realized he couldn't pass up an opportunity to be the first in his family to graduate from college. He completed his studies with an undergraduate degree in criminal justice.

He was also a leader on the Crimson Tide's defense with a core group of friends and mentors from Alabama that will last a lifetime. He was particularly close with outside linebacker Ryan Anderson, wide receiver Calvin Ridley, Harrison, and his position coach, Derrick Ansley. "Man, DA is cool," Jackson said. "I can talk to him about anything. There's so much more than football."

Jackson II and Blair went so far as to say that the Jackson of his high school years wouldn't recognize the man he became in Tuscaloosa. "It's absolutely gratifying," Blair said during Eddie's tenure at UA. "Coming from the demographic that he comes from and the neighborhood that he comes from, a lot of guys ain't coming out from there. He's an absolute success story.

"It's gratifying for me to see the four-and-a-half-year development of the guy I once knew. He's not the same kid that he once was on signing day. That dude is a whole other man. He's got perspective. He understands where he wants to be in the next three to four years, and we're talking about somebody who didn't even have a goal for what was going to happen next month."

All in all, the struggles are what make the successes all the sweeter, Jackson said. Without them, he wouldn't fully appreciate how good life is. He still wishes he had been healthy at the end of 2016. He thinks the season would've ended differently. Still, he knows everything happens for a reason. "It got a little frustrating, but I always kept faith in God and my family," Jackson said. "They stayed on top of me and kept pushing me and had faith in me. It was valuable to me to be the underdog, and now I'm making noise."

Acknowledgments

I WANT TO THANK MY FATHER FOR GIVING ME A LOVE OF THIS wonderful, crazy sport that I've made my wonderful life. I've never known a world where I didn't have a game to watch on a beautiful fall afternoon, and I hope I never do.

I owe a debt of gratitude to my wife, Stephanie, who puts up with me being gone all fall. I've missed more weddings and birthdays than I can remember, and she represents our family because it's known that "Aaron's at a game." She is my rock and my biggest believer. Everyone needs a support system like the one she gives me. I love you more with each passing day, and I can't thank you enough for sacrificing so that I could finish this book. I can't believe I've been lucky enough to find someone to love a man like me.

To Grayson, who's brought me more joy than I thought possible. You are a ray of light, and I pray you always will be.

To Scout, you taught me responsibility when that's exactly what I needed.

To Bill and Sharon, who've shown me what family is. I cannot begin to repay the love and unconditional support you've given to me.

To Trey, Kelsey, Coleman, and Berkley, I love you all.

To Eric, I hope you know that I'll always be there for you.

To David, who took a chance on an unknown kid.

To Tommy, who recognized something in that kid and gave him opportunity after opportunity.

To Cecil, who always treated me as an equal even though I never was. Your friendship through the years was always an amazing thing in my life. Thank you for trusting me. Thank you for valuing me. Thank you for letting me into your circle. I can never repay what you taught me.

To Marc, you're one hell of a friend. Whether it's over bourbon or just a quick conversation via text, your friendship means the world to me. I cannot express how proud I am of you. From JN 311 to road trips to Missouri and Memphis, a bond was made that travels from Brooklyn to Alabama.

To Caleb, thanks, buddy, for always making me laugh. I can always count on you to remind me how much my favorite teams suck. I hope our sons one day share a basketball court.

To Matt, thanks for always letting me bounce ideas off you, even when I'm rambling and not making much sense.

To Wesley, I haven't known you the longest, but you came along at the perfect time for me. Your outgoing personality and ability to welcome me into your group have added a certain spirit to my life. I hope our friendship continues.

To Jimmy, I hope you know how good you are at this. I've been excited to see your progression. You transitioned careers at a scary time. Congrats on chasing your dreams. Thanks for being one of my biggest supporters.

To Jimbo, you are one of my favorite people.

To Josh, I know I sometimes drive you crazy. It hasn't always been easy, but we've reached a good place. Thanks for all your assistance throughout the years.

To my mawmaw, I literally wouldn't be here without you. You were the first person in my life to show me what unconditional love was. You taught me to reach higher, to never settle for the hand life dealt you. You are at the forefront of my mind for every major life event. I wish you were here to meet my wife and your great-grandson. I miss you. I love you.